DATE DUE

MAY 0 5 2006	
OCT 2 5 2007	

MARRIAGE & DIVORCE

J. VERNON McGEE

Publishers Since 1798

THOMAS NELSON PUBLISHERS
Nashville

Published in Nashville, Tennessee, by Thomas Nelson, Inc.

Library of Congress Cataloging-in-Publication Data

McGee, J. Vernon (John Vernon), 1904–1988
  Marriage and divorce / J. Vernon McGee.
    p. cm.
  ISBN 0-7852-7454-5
  1. Marriage—Biblical teaching.   2. Divorce—Biblical teaching.   I. Title.
BS680.M35M35 1998
234'.165—dc21   97–36461
                                            CIP

Printed in the United States of America
1 2 3 4 5 6 7 BVG 03 02 01 00 99 98

CONTENTS

INTRODUCTION

Fairy tales and romances always seem to end with the bright and rosy picture of a future filled with happiness and bliss. Actually, they end where life really begins—at the marriage ceremony. Why is it that today about half of marriages end in divorce? Obviously, couples are not living happily ever after. Some don't make it through the honeymoon, while others manage to hold on for a year or so before giving up.

J. Vernon McGee was deeply concerned by the escalating divorce rate in America. He did not write on the subject, in view of the scores of books coming off the press that seemed to deal with the issue adequately.

However, he found himself doing more and more marriage counseling with members of his own congregation and therefore devoted several helpful sermons to his entire flock. Each of these messages now comprises a chapter in this book.

Most of the current books on marriage and divorce put down certain rules and regulations that are supposed to make marriage a success. Either that, or they focus only on the issue of sex. Dr. McGee, on the other hand, takes a simpler approach—what does the Bible say about it?

The real problem is not divorce; the problem is marriage. People are getting married who are not prepared for a relationship that God alone can bless. The correction should be made before marriage rather than trying to patch things up afterward. The old bromide is still accurate: A ounce of prevention is worth a pound of cure.

It takes the right kind of man and the right kind of woman to build a happy marriage. Only a Spirit-filled man can be the head of his home. Only a Spirit-filled woman can respond to a Spirit-filled man. Anything less ensures a rough voyage over the sea of matrimony.

CHAPTER 1

ARE MARRIAGES MADE IN HEAVEN OR ELSEWHERE?

There is today an unwarranted assumption that marriage is a matter about which God adopts a hands-off policy, that the choosing of a husband or wife is not any business of the church because the Bible is outmoded on the subject of modern marriage. It is also assumed that a preacher should not invade this area but should leave it to the novelist, to the stage, and to the screen.

I was interested in hearing what was said by a couple of ladies who stopped in front of our church's bulletin board to read the title of this message— "Are Marriages Made in Heaven or Elsewhere?" One of them said to the other (not realizing who I was standing beside them), "Well, I wonder what *he* thinks *he* knows about it!" So at the outset let me assure you that I'm not attempting to sit in the place of a Dr. Know-It-All or walk with a presumptuous step. But I am attempting to say something that might be helpful, especially to young people who are getting ready to make this most important commitment of marriage, and also to provide something to strengthen the home life of this generation.

The psychologist and the social worker today are considered experts while God is considered just an amateur! I know of nothing over which God exercises more influence and about which He has more concern than marriage. He claims to be the only authority who can solve this today, and it is time that He is heard!

Southern California, where I live, has become a national disgrace by the number of aberrant lifestyles—for which our children are paying an awful price. Those of us today who are expected to solve the problems of the human family find that we are interviewing more and more people along this line. Oh, my friend, the world is caving in as far as the home is concerned. And the home is collapsing! Multitudes today are experiencing shipwrecks upon the sea of matrimony.

Two weeks ago a lady whom I judged was past sixty—I don't like to judge any lady to be past sixty, but I do believe this one was—came to me for counseling. When she came into my study and sat down, there was an air of refinement about her, and culture and education. As she sat there I said to myself, "Well, at least here is somebody who is not going to talk about a broken marriage." Well, in thirty seconds she started telling me her problem, and it was the same story! Whether it's a girl of eighteen or sixty-eight, it seems today that a broken home is the great theme. And that's one of the reasons we are turning our attention to this subject. God does have something to say about it. Let me remind you that God had Abraham send his servant all the way into the land of Haran to find a bride for his son. Getting a God-fearing wife for his son was very important to Abraham, and God was superintending the whole mission, and the servant said, "I being in the way, the Lord led me."

My friend, if there's ever a time when you and I need to be walking in the Lord's way, it's during that time of choosing someone to walk with us through life. Multitudes who have had an unfortunate voyage on the troubled waters of matrimony have become bitter, pessimistic, sarcastic, and resentful, and as a result caustic remarks are voiced. Someone has said that "marriage is love's hangover." And another has defined a bachelor as a man who does not make the same mistake once. The story is told of a Scotsman who came to this country. In clearing customs, one of the questions asked him was, "Who is this woman with you?" He said, "It's my wife." The customs officer said, "Can you prove that she's your wife?" Old Scotty thought a moment, then said, "I'll give you ten pounds if you can prove she's not." I tell you, friends, these are the things that are coming out of bitter experiences.

I had one of the greatest shocks of my ministry following one of the first funerals I conducted. The deceased had been, for many years, the wife of a now elderly man, and I attempted to eulogize her. Well, from that day to this I've never again eulogized at a funeral. I had attempted to say what a wonderful wife she'd been and what a wonderful mother she'd been. But coming back from the funeral I rode in the car with this man—he and I were the only two passengers—and we rode along for about five minutes in silence. Then he turned and said to me, "Vernon, I thank God that I've buried that woman." I tell you, that was a shock for a young preacher, especially one who had looked at marriage through rose-colored glasses.

My beloved, there are many such tragedies lining the highway today. How I would like to spare someone such a tragedy and to be helpful to others who are headed in the same direction. Some folk say that marriages are made in heaven. While it is true that some marriages are made in heaven, there are others that obviously were not made there. God wants *your* marriage to be made in heaven, and if you let Him, He will make the arrangements.

There's at least one marriage in the Scripture— I think there are more—that obviously was made in heaven. It's not debatable, because God arranged it all. In fact, it was God who provided the bride for this first man. It was the marriage of Adam and Eve. And in their marriage, my beloved, you'll find great principles that are put down for a successful marriage. They've never been altered, updated, or changed. And the reason is that human nature never changes. For instance, my grandfather proposed to my grandmother as they rode in a buggy. My father proposed to my mother on a passenger train and I did the same thing in a

Chevrolet automobile. But it was the same sort of experience that grandfather had, that father had, and that son had. Now the great principles that God laid down are simple and certain principles, but they've been largely ignored in our day. And when they're ignored and not obeyed, tragedy strikes with all of its force coming in like a Texas tornado. I believe if there's one place where the Scripture absolutely applies, it's in marriage. In Galatians 6:7 the Word of God says, "Do not be deceived, God is not mocked; for whatever a man sows, that he will also reap." I want you to note in this marriage of Adam and Eve these great principles: the *foundation of marriage,* the *function of marriage*, and the *fulfillment of marriage.*

The Foundation of Marriage

Consider these three verses in Genesis 2, and I want you to notice, first of all, the foundation of marriage:

And the LORD God said, "It is not good that man should be alone; I will make him a helper comparable to him." Out of the ground the LORD God formed every beast of the field and every bird of the air, and brought them to Adam to see what he would call them. And whatever Adam called each living creature, that was its name. So Adam gave names to all cattle, to the birds of the air, and to every beast of the field. But for Adam there was not

found a helper comparable to him. (verses 18–20)

Now, my beloved, the simple explanation of marriage found in verse 20 is expressed in very few words: God brought Eve to Adam that he might have a helpmeet. Actually Eve was more than a helpmeet or helper, she was the one to complete Adam as a person. That was God's primary purpose. That's the very foundation of marriage.

One day a young man came to talk to me, an attractive young fellow and a fine Christian who was studying for the ministry. He had met a young lady who was just as attractive as he was. He said to me, "I've fallen madly in love with her, and we want to get married."

"Are you sure you're in love?"

"Yes, I'm positive I'm in love."

"How do you know?"

"I just can't live without her!"

"Well, Brother, when you get like that, it's time to get married—when you can't live without her!" God intended for that to be the very foundation of marriage. Man is only half a man by himself. Woman is only half a woman by herself. Man, with all of his strength and all of his ability and all of his boasting today, cannot propagate himself. So God brought this lovely creature to Adam that she might be his other half. God did not have a companion for man in the angelic host; neither did He have a companion for him in the animal world.

To me one of the tragedies of southern California is to see so many people who have a little dog on a leash, and that's all they have to love. I say this honestly: I feel sorry for them. The other evening I took my little girl for a walk when it was just getting dark, and I heard someone speaking. I've never heard such lovey-dovey language in my life, and I took my little girl by the hand, thinking we were interfering with something, and I started to tiptoe off. Then I saw a lady who lived in the neighborhood pick up a little dog in her arms and walk off down the block. Oh, how my heart goes out to a person like that.

Adam couldn't find a companion in the animal world below him or in the angelic world above him, and he was lonesome. Then God brought to him this woman that she might be his companion. When a woman or a man does not prove to be a helper to the other, then that person is failing in the very foundation of marriage itself.

I remember during the Texas Centennial that every time I went on those fairgrounds I went right by a statue placed near the entrance. It was a statue of a pioneer man as he stood there, strong and stalwart, lean and muscled, and by his side was a little woman wearing a sunbonnet. She barely reached his shoulder, and they had a little child between them. I stopped and looked at that statue every time I went there. And as I studied it I thought, *That's the type of manhood and womanhood that made America.* And it's the type that made Texas, if you please. Those pioneers who came, strong and stalwart, and many of them Christian, found in each other a close companionship, one helping the other.

It reminded me of a rancher I knew in west Texas when I was a boy. He was a huge, rugged rancher out there who always impressed me because even when he came to church he wore boots with spurs on them. And when he'd come into the church wearing those jingling star spurs, you could hear them all over the place. If the preacher was speaking, he would just have to stop until that brother sat down! Big fellow that he was, by his side always was his little woman in a sunbonnet. He told the story of how they came west in a covered wagon. They were not prosperous in those early days. They had come out there as a young married couple, had raised a large family, and God had wonderfully blessed them. She was one of the sweetest persons I've ever met. But the story went that when the Indians attacked one night, while he did the shooting, she did the loading. She was a part of him, and she stood beside him through thick and thin.

How different from many today who, at the first provocation or difficulty that arises, will run home to Mama. At the first conflict in the home, they throw the marriage overboard and decide that it is not for them. One of the reasons that so many go to the divorce courts is just simply this: They're not equipped for marriage. They're not equipped for the new relationship of being helpers one to the other. They can't resolve conflict, my beloved. As soon as she burns the biscuits the first time, the honeymoon is over. You have probably heard about the young wife who made biscuits for the first time and proudly served them to her husband—and then she began to cry. He asked her, "What are you crying for?" She sobbed, "You fed them to the *dog*!" And he said, "Ah, don't cry. The dog is still alive!" I tell you, friend, those are the things today that upset a marriage. God's intention is that a husband and wife be helpers to one another.

A young soldier boy who attended the church I served during the war had been stationed nearby, and he came to see me after the war was over. I had never seen a young fellow as sad as he was, and I said to him, "You ought to be very happy to be returning home." His reply was, "Dr. McGee, I'm the most unhappy man in this world. I've come in to talk with you. When I left the battlefield I had been killing men, and I came home to kill one more man. I heard that my wife had been untrue to me, and I was going to kill this man, but since I've been here the past few weeks and attending the services, God has melted my heart so I don't think I'm going through with it." I said, "No, I wouldn't either. I don't think she's worth it. And I don't think he's worth it. Don't let a murder ruin the rest of your life." Then I asked him, "Where did you meet her?" He said, "I met her on the dance floor." "Well," I said, "you can't expect it to work out in any other way than it has."

You can't start the thing wrong and have it turn out right, my beloved. God says the very foundation of marriage is that each one must be a helper to the other. That's the foundation that God has laid.

I think of that lovely story of Nathaniel Hawthorne. He was employed as a port officer at the Port of Boston during the administration of Van Buren. And when Van Buren left office, he lost his position. He came home very much discouraged and despondent. As he sat slumped in a chair, his wife went to get pen and paper, which she put before him, and she whispered in his ear, "Now you can do what you've always wanted to do. You can write." And from that moment on, he began to develop his talent and gained international fame for his masterpiece, *The Scarlet Letter*. Why? Because he had a wonderful helper next to him! That's the basis, the very foundation of marriage, when both husband and wife have that loving care for one another.

The Function of Marriage

And now I want you to consider briefly the function of marriage. Note with me two more verses:

And the LORD God caused a deep sleep to fall on Adam, and he slept; and He took one of his ribs, and closed up the flesh in its place. Then the rib which the LORD God had taken from man He made into a woman, and He brought her to the man. (Genesis 2:21–22)

I think that's one of the loveliest stories in the Scriptures. Eve was taken from Adam's side, from right next to his heart, to be his equal and to walk with him. Notice that it says God "brought her to the man." She must have been a wonderful person, for she came from the very hand of God Himself. May I say again, my beloved, that God wants you—especially if you are a young person—to let Him guide you in choosing the one that's to walk by your side through life.

From the beginning God never permitted His people to go outside their own people to marry someone whose faith was unlike theirs. Have you ever noticed that? For instance, note God's condemnation of Balaam (Numbers 22) for enticing Israel to sin by intermarrying with the heathen around them and then turning to heathen idols. Generations before, God had sent this man Jacob back to the land of Haran that he might get a bride. And may I emphasize that it was not *racial* discrimination; it was for religious reasons. This is confirmed in the case of Ruth the Moabitess, in the case of Rahab the harlot, and in the case of Tamar. They were all outsiders, but God permitted His people to marry them because they had become believers. It was always for a religious reason that God forbade His people to marry outsiders.

An illustration of the seriousness of intermarriage took place in the days of Nehemiah. He was the instrument God used for one of the greatest revivals in history. Nehemiah was a great reformer because reformation follows revival. One of the things that he did was to reform the home life of God's people. They were intermarrying with unbelievers, and this man Nehemiah used what may seem to us to be extreme measures!

> **In those days I also saw Jews who had married women of Ashdod, Ammon, and Moab. And half of their children spoke the language of Ashdod, and could not speak the language of Judah, but spoke according to the language of one or the other people. So I contended with them and cursed them, struck some of them and pulled out their hair, and made them swear by God, saying, "You shall not give your daughters as wives to their sons, nor take their daughters for your sons or yourselves. . . . Should we then hear of your doing all this great evil, transgressing against our God by marrying pagan women?"** (Nehemiah 13:23–25, 27)

If there's one thing today that's clear in Scripture— and I'll emphasize it with all the force I can muster— it's this: Young person, if you are a Christian, do *not* marry an unbeliever! I think of the tragedy in homes—tragedies not from alcohol, although there's enough from that, but from marriages between believers and unbelievers! I would say that at least 50 percent of the cases that come to me are those that have been caused by the marriage of an unbeliever to a believer.

Certainly when God took this woman from the side and near the heart of Adam, He was indicating that He intended for her to be his spiritual as well as his physical equal and to walk with him in a personal relationship with God. The home that you, my friend, establish will be lived on the plane of the partner who lives at the *lowest* spiritual level. Certainly there should be unity in a marriage and agreement along spiritual lines. There must be something to hold the husband and wife together on the spiritual plane, and the starting point for holding them together on that spiritual plane is for both of them to be believers.

An early tragedy in David's life was his marriage to Michal, the daughter of Saul. David, in his boundless joy and fervor that the ark of the covenant was being brought up to Jerusalem, exhibited a great deal of emotion. And when he did, the record tells us:

And it happened, as the ark of the covenant of the LORD came to the City of David, that Michal, Saul's daughter, looked through a window and saw King David whirling and playing music; and she despised him in her heart. (1 Chronicles 15:29)

And as you know, that sharp division on spiritual matters has been repeated thousands of times since then.

It may amaze you for me to say that I find more saved boys marrying unsaved girls than the other way around. A young man came to talk with me about getting married, and he had decided to marry a very beautiful girl, but she was an unbeliever. In fact, she was a professional dancer. And I told him, "No, I'll not perform the ceremony at all." And may I say to you, that's one thing I'm sure about—I'll never marry a believer to an unbeliever if I know it. They'll have to deceive me in order to get me to marry them. I think it's one of the greatest tragedies that can happen in this hour in which we are living, and I do not want to have any part in it at all. This young man insisted, "Oh, Dr. McGee, we can make a go of it." I said, "I don't think you can. You know Scripture says you're not to separate what God has joined together. And, Brother, it works both ways. You can't join together what God has separated, either. You are a Christian, you're on the way to heaven, she's on the way to hell. And I tell you that *God* is going to divorce you someday. So how in the world do you expect to make a go of it with one being a Christian and the other being a non-Christian?"

Last Tuesday night two hundred young graduates walked across the platform of our church. I suppose everyone thought of them as happy young people. May I say that one of those young men was far from happy, and I doubt there are half a dozen people who know this. His wife has left him. His wife says now that she's not a Christian, never was a Christian, although she professed it one Sunday morning after I preached about a year ago. She was a student at a fine Bible school and since then has graduated from that school. But now she says she's not a Christian! And this young husband has found that she's been running around with another man. She has left him now. How my heart goes out to that young man, a fine student, an attractive young fellow, and a man of ability who can be used of God.

But what a tragedy has come to him! I asked him, "Do you mind if I tell your story?" "No," he said. "If it can help any young person, Dr. McGee, you tell it to try to warn them from this!" Oh, young person, make dead sure the person you marry is a genuine Christian! Make that your first priority above everything else, and save yourself from a tragic life.

We've all thought of Mark Twain as a humorist, yet Mark Twain's life was one of tragedy. Mark Twain married a girl by the name of Olivia Langdon. She was an attractive young lady and a Christian. And she had questioned Mark Twain—whose name, as you know, was Samuel Clemens. Calling him by his nickname, she said, "Uel, you're a Christian, aren't you?" He loved her so much that he was willing to promise anything. Mark Twain said, "Yes, I'm a Christian," and went with her to church and continued to go with her to church until one day after they had been married for about two years. He came in after the service and said to her, "Livvy, I can't go on with it any longer. I can't go on with the farce. I'm not a Christian. You can go on, but I can't."

So she stuck by him. By that time Mark Twain was becoming famous. He was invited to Europe, and she went with him. She was able to hold her own in society, but they were moving with a skeptical and fast group. While they were abroad an awful tragedy came to them—their oldest daughter, Susy, died of meningitis. The grief was unimaginable. When they returned home he came into her room and said, "Livvy, if your Christian faith gives you any comfort, turn to it." And with tears streaming down her face she said, "Uel, I don't have any more Christian faith, it's all gone now." And their lives turned to ashes. The tragedy of a humorist! Oh, my beloved, "Do not be deceived, God is not mocked; for whatever a man sows, that he will also reap" (Galatians 6:7).

The Fulfillment of Marriage

Let me mention just this last point, the fulfillment of marriage. Being together, experiencing oneness in heart, mind, and body, carries with it tremendous fulfillment. Do you notice that in Genesis 5:2 God called *them* Adam (meaning *mankind*), and He did not call them the Adamses? They are one. They're made one flesh, and they are obviously one flesh in the child. In the Genesis account God says, "Therefore a man shall leave his father and mother and be joined to his wife. . ." (Genesis 2:24).

Let me give you another good principle. Young person, when you get married, the tie between husband and wife is so strong in God's sight that it will break even the tie of natural relationships—if necessary. May I say, the second thing that is troubling more marriages than anything else is the interference of in-laws. God says that "a man shall *leave* his father and mother and be joined to his wife." Start on your own! Don't be dependent on Papa and Mama if you want to make a happy home and a successful marriage. When God brought to Adam this woman whom He had created for him, he chose to stay with her. In fact, he chose to stay with her even on that day when she came to him and said, "I have eaten of the tree." She could have been driven out of the garden for disobeying her Creator, and Adam could have stayed there alone. But he didn't stay alone. He took the forbidden fruit, choosing to go with the woman that God had given him.

Oh, my friend, today there is One who came down to this earth, Jesus, our Kinsman Redeemer who actually gave Himself in full payment for our sins. He came down from heaven because of His love for us and identified Himself with us in order that we might be joined to Him for eternity.

Are you on the threshold of marriage, but you're not sure of your standing or the other person's standing before the Lord? Beloved, let me put up the red signal and say to you, *"Stop! Look! Listen!"* before you take that step. You may say, "It's too late now—our wedding plans are already finalized." No, sir, it's not too late until the knot is tied. It's better to say *no* now than to say *Reno* a little later on. And I tell you, you're going to say it unless you begin a marriage on the one foundation God has given, that is, the foundation of a marriage between one man and one woman who are genuine believers, and the establishment of a Christian home.

CHAPTER 2

SO YOU WANT TO GET MARRIED

There was a time when I could not have given this message. However, God has graciously opened my eyes to a new dimension in this area, and He has also provided mercifully an inspiration and impetus that I might do it.

It is still true to say that there are three major events in the life of every person—birth, marriage, and death. You and I had nothing in the world to do with our birth. We just found ourselves the center of attraction! And the date of death for any individual actually cannot be determined—even a suicide is not always successful.

But the one event in the life of an individual over which he or she does have some control is marriage. The fact of the matter is, he or she has everything to do with the marriage. God gives to each individual a free will and it is in marriage that free will can be exercised as in no other area of life. God places, therefore, total responsibility on the individual who gets married. That's the reason He will not permit the marriage tie to be broken. The exceptions are only on certain well- defined conditions according to His Word. And if a child of God is to follow the Word of God, he will certainly have to follow it in this particular connection. Marriage is the one human relationship that God has promised to bless above all others (see Genesis 1:27–28).

It is very interesting that Scripture doesn't tell us of the Lord Jesus going to the groundbreaking ceremonies for the temple or for new buildings or for a new subdivision in Jerusalem. But He did go over a hill to a marriage in Cana of Galilee, and that's where He began His ministry. My friend, that was no accident.

When marriage is made in the framework that God has fixed, happiness will inevitably ensue. When it's made outside that framework, unspeakable sorrow and tragedy will come. Therefore, the choosing of a husband or a wife is the biggest business that any of us can engage in—it's the biggest business and the most significant event of a person's life. The making of a home is the most important accomplishment that anyone can have down here.

Now there is a strange anomaly today. Men and women are trained for years to enter upon a business career. A professional career requires years of specialized training. Yet preparation for marriage, the most momentous and important part of one's life, is almost entirely, if not totally, neglected today.

May I be very personal? I spent nine years preparing for the ministry. I didn't spend nine minutes preparing to get married! And may I say that in spite of the fact that I'm a poor preacher, I'm a better preacher than I am a husband or a father. And this is due to the background that most of us have had and the lack of emphasis upon this most important part of life. Of course, today it is getting a great deal of attention.

Nevertheless, most young people today are absolutely unprepared for marriage. It would be criminal to send a couple of landlubbers out in a rowboat on a storm-tossed sea without chart or compass. Yet month after month young people are being sent out on the sea of matrimony without any preparation for or realization of the real meaning of marriage. Little wonder today that they are making a shipwreck of marriage and a shipwreck of their lives!

As I write, the local paper is running a series on "The Divorce Crisis," as they call it. Well, that is like locking the stable after the horse is gone. May I say to you, the problem today is not divorce, the problem is marriage—people getting married who are not prepared for it at all.

The Ideal Christian Marriage

I am confining this message to Christian marriage; that is, God's ideal for the believer today. Personally, I have never knowingly married a believer to an unbeliever. If I do not know the couple personally and don't know of their conversion, it's the question I always ask first: Is this to be a marriage between a believer and an unbeliever? And if it is, I will not have a part in that at all.

Therefore, since I am talking about the marriage of two believers, I want to consider four specific passages of Scripture that are relevant to this subject. So let's go back to that which is basic, and it is this passage in Genesis, the creation of the man and of the woman. I've given a great deal of time to the restudy of this passage because of the attention given to the subject and the alarming breakup of marriage today, even among Christians. I want to know what God had in mind when He created them. Notice this:

 And the LORD God said, "It is not good that man should be alone; I will make him a helper comparable to him." (Genesis 2:18)

Now apparently God created man and left him alone in the Garden of Eden for a period of time before He created Eve and brought her to him. Now why did God do that? Well, I think there was a twofold reason. The first was so the man might become aware of his need, and then, so he might have an appreciation of the woman when she was brought to him. To me, those two things are obvious. God did not create the woman at the beginning. He first put the man in the garden alone.

And God did something else there—He had man name all of the animals. This reveals the high intelligence of Adam. If you think he was some sort of caveman, you are entirely wrong. He was more intelligent than any person here today, because you and I get our intelligence from him, and none of us is going to come up to Adam's level, as far as an IQ is concerned.

Out of the ground the Lord God formed [the word is *molded*] **every beast of the field and every bird of the air, and brought them to Adam to see what he would call them. And whatever Adam called each living creature, that was its name.**

Notice the intelligence of this first man:

So Adam gave names to all cattle, to the birds of the air, and to every beast of the field. But for Adam there was not found a helper comparable to him. (Genesis 2:19–20)

Two things happened here. First, man revealed his intelligence in being able to name these animals. You talk about being a biologist—this man Adam was a biologist; he knew these animals. And having named them, Adam made another discovery. In the entire animal world there was no human being to be a companion for him. The word *helpmeet* or *helper,* as several versions translate it, doesn't quite convey the meaning that is here. The Hebrew word is *heser*, and if you want to get at the root of it, it means this: God made this woman, and she was to *agree* to Adam, agreeing to him, answering to him, compensating for him. Man had no equal in the animal world, and he certainly had none in the angelic world. Therefore God, during this lapse of time, let man see that he needed someone who would be a complement to him.

You see, man was created a social creature, and God would come down and have fellowship with him. Friend, Adam was no robot. He didn't bow down because God pushed a button. Adam bowed because he was given a free will, and he did it willingly and gladly. God wanted that kind of creature.

Then God made the woman, and a very lovely statement is made:

> **And the LORD God caused a deep sleep to fall on Adam, and he slept; and He took one of his ribs, and closed up the flesh in its place. Then the rib which the LORD God had taken from man He made into a woman, and He brought her to the man.** (Genesis 2:21–22)

God had "molded" the animals, but the thought here is of an artist producing a masterpiece, if you please, and that is exactly what this first woman was. Eve was a masterpiece. As one fellow said, "A woman ought to be better-looking than a man. After all, God practiced on man first, and woman was His second edition." And certainly He had had an opportunity to "practice" on man. But the thought here is that He did make the loveliest creature that possibly could be made.

> **And Adam said:**
> **"This is now bone of my bones**

And flesh of my flesh;
She shall be called Woman,
Because she was taken out of Man."
(Genesis 2:23)

The Hebrew word for man is *ish* and the word for woman is *isha*. Notice the similarity, which we do not have in English. He says, "I'm ish, and she's isha; she is part of me." Let's not miss what the Hebrew has here.

My friend, do you know what marriage actually is? Marriage is putting the rib back in its place. That's what I intend to do at a wedding. I like to feel that I'm performing a surgical procedure that is more delicate than any surgeon ever performed, putting a rib back in place. Why? Because man was created to be a social creature, but he was alone and became aware of that loneliness. So God brings to him the other part of him! Now that is the picture the Scripture gives of the marriage ceremony.

The Wife of Your Youth

Centuries later the prophet Malachi brings God's charge against the nation Israel, telling why He has judged them:

And this is the second thing you do:
You cover the altar of the LORD with tears,
With weeping and crying;
So He does not regard the offering anymore,

Nor receive it with goodwill from your hands.
(Malachi 2:13)

Imagine this: They were coming before God in that day, actually shedding tears and making offerings, and they were saying, "Why doesn't God receive us, and why doesn't He bless us?" And, beloved, this may give you an inkling of why God is not blessing the church today. Notice this:

Yet you say, "For what reason?"
Because the LORD has been witness
Between you and the wife of your youth,
With whom you have dealt treacherously;
Yet she is your companion
And your wife by covenant.
But did He not make them one,
Having a remnant of the Spirit?
And why one?
He seeks godly offspring.
Therefore take heed to your spirit,
And let none deal
Treacherously with the wife of his youth.
(Malachi 2:14–15)

They had overlooked the fact that when God created this woman, He didn't make a harem for Adam, one wife from each rib, but God made only one Eve. The thought is that in marriage God intended that there be one man and one woman. What a lesson there is in that. How this day and generation needs to understand that principle!

I believe God has one special mate for each believer and I think you'll find as you read the rest of this chapter and book that I can back it up with the Word of God. I do not say that he or she always marries that individual. But I do believe that God has in our day one person for each individual. Now you may say, "That's being a romantic!" No, that's not romanticism at all, it is God's practical truth.

Till Death Do Us Part?

There are two or three popular phrases in the marriage ceremony that I do not use. For instance, I never say, "Until death do us part." Do you know why? I don't think death will separate a couple in a marriage that God has really joined together. I think they are going to be together in eternity. Why not? Somebody says, "But Jesus said they're not married in heaven!" and they quote Matthew 22:30: "For in the resurrection they neither marry nor are given in marriage, but are like angels of God in heaven." True, people don't get married up there, they do it down here. But if they want to, they can be together up there.

Now you may say to me again, "You are being very romantic." No, God is very specific. He says, "I have given you one wife. I have given you one husband. That is My ideal for you." The problem today is that there are too many girls and too many boys who are anxious to get married, and they get somebody else before they get the one whom God has for them. Only God can make the right choice at the time of marriage. This is the reason a child of God should stay in close fellowship with God, especially when courting! That's when you need Him to direct you in making the most important decision of life.

Submit? Obey? Who, Me?

A passage of Scripture that I consider all-important in the subject of marriage is Ephesians 5. In verse 21 Paul says, "Submitting to one another in the fear of God." This entire section goes back to the command in verse 18 to be filled with the Spirit. Paul is talking now to Spirit-filled believers. And Spirit-filled believers should manifest this: "Submitting to one another in the fear of God."

Now I have news for you if you are one who argues about this point in the following verse, "Wives, submit to your own husbands, as to the Lord." To begin with, in the better manuscripts the word *submit* doesn't even occur. It shouldn't be here. Somebody may say, "Well, we need a verb." Yes, we do. "And shouldn't we bring down the verb *submitting*?" I think it is quite proper to do so, but we do need to understand that the Holy Spirit was not the one who put it there, and neither did the apostle Paul put it there. That, in and of itself, ought to alert us.

Submit does not mean obey. In a marriage ceremony I have never used the word *obey* for the woman.

Then where do people get that? Some will say, "The Bible says 'submit.'" Yes, but what does *submit* really mean?

A big bully called me some years ago. At that time he was a member of my church. He said, "I want you to tell my wife that she is to obey me."

I said, "I'll do nothing of the kind."

"Well, the Bible says she should, and you're a preacher, aren't you?"

"Yes, I'm a preacher, but the Bible does not say that. My brother, nowhere does the Bible tell any woman to obey a big, brutal bully. You cannot find that in the Word of God."

Love: How It Works

Notice that we are talking about Spirit-filled people here, and *submit*, as we are going to see in just a moment, means something. What kind of husband are we talking about?

Wives, submit to your own husbands, as to the Lord. . . . Husbands, love your wives, just as Christ also loved the church and gave Himself for her. (Ephesians 5:22, 25)

Will you think carefully with me now—God commanded the husband to love his wife, but He never did command a wife to love her husband! Yes, she is to love him, but let's see how.

God created her as a helper—agreeing to and answering to her husband. "Husbands, love your wives." And when you love your wife, what does she do? She answers, "I love you." If he loves, she loves. If he is gentle, she responds. If he is kind, if he is considerate, then she responds to love. If he is brutal, she will strike back. She is to "agree" to him. When you tell me, husband, that you are having trouble with your wife, the chances are the trouble lies with you.

Man is the aggressor, he initiates the action. Even God had this in mind when He made man and woman physically. Man delivers, the woman receives. God says that man is the one always to initiate the action. He says, "I love you," and she answers, "I love you." It can't be otherwise, my beloved.

Look at the Song of Solomon, for you have there a great story of human love. Here is what the bridegroom says in chapter 1 verse 15: "Behold, you are fair, my love! Behold, you are fair!" Isn't that lovely? Oh, it's not very original, but it sure is wonderful when you mean it! And he says that to her, his bride. Now is she going to come back with something really novel? No. Listen to her: "Behold, you are handsome, my beloved!" What is she doing? She is responding with the same thing he said to her—which is exactly what God said she is to do. She is to answer to the man. And it must be that way if there is to be blessing!

Now *submit* is the Greek word *hypostasis*. *Hypo* is the preposition, meaning "under;" *stasis* means "to stand." So *hypostasis* means "to stand under." In other words, it literally means "to look up to," and I personally do not think any woman ought to marry a man that she can't look up to. A woman needs to be able to say, "I respect that man, I look up to him, I admire him, I have confidence in him, I can trust myself to him." Then, all other things being equal, when and if he says, "I love you," she is going to answer, "I love you."

My friend, the caveman stuff is out. In fact, it never was in. And certainly it is not according to the Word of God. No woman will respond positively to that kind of treatment. The purple passion of Hollywood is not God's ideal either. The woman is to respond to the man always. That is the picture presented in the Word of God.

Effective Sex Education

Now somebody is going to say to me, "I have found a verse of Scripture in Titus that does say something about the woman loving the man." Yes, but have you noticed how it says it? When Paul wrote to a young preacher, he said, "I want you to instruct the older women, those who are reverent believers and have had experience, that they may train the young women to love their husbands, to love their children."

Does it mean that the older women are to train young wives to love their husbands? Yes, because this is something God did not command at the beginning. Therefore Paul said they are to receive training. And this is my reason, as we will see in a moment, for thinking that at the beginning the success of the marriage is entirely in the hands of the man. This older woman with her experience and wisdom is to teach the young woman to love her husband, and it is not sex education. Love and sex are not synonymous at all. I believe we need to recognize that today in a very special way. I read an amazing article written by Julian Huxley, an outstanding biologist and admitted athiest. He wrote a course on evolution and the modern synthesis and declared that God has nothing to do with this universe. Yet he has also penned this:

> There is a distinction between love and sex. Sexual desire by itself is lust. It is universally regarded as immoral, but for true lovers the act of physical union is motivated not merely by desire for pleasure, but for the transcendent sense of total union which it can bring.

That statement comes closer to biblical truth than a great many articles I've read in Christian magazines.

May I say to you that sex without love is animal activity. But love, my friend, makes sex a holy and sacred act of consecration for believers. It is the time when they truly become one and can see something of that holy union between Christ and their own selves.

In Marriage Only

Now we will look at 1 Corinthians, the seventh chapter. We often misunderstand this passage because we do not understand the background. Paul is answering a letter the Corinthians sent to him:

Now concerning the things of which you wrote to me: It is good for a man not to touch a woman. (verse 1)

What does Paul mean by that?

Well, we need to recognize that Paul wrote this against the black background of the most depraved and degrading paganism imaginable. The sexual practices of the Corinthians had destroyed the glory of Greece. You will find that sex and religion were the same thing in Corinth. At certain seasons they had what were known as "fertility rites" in the temple. And in that temple to Aphrodite (or Venus) in the city of Corinth there were one thousand so-called "vestal virgins" who were nothing in the world but temple prostitutes. Every man, regardless of whether he was married or not, participated in the temple rites during that particular period.

It was the new believers in that environment to whom Paul was writing. Many of these Gentiles who were converted came out of this raw heathenism. They had no Bible instruction as do Christians of today. The point of their question was, "When these ceremonies come around, should we go into the heathen temple?" Paul says no, it is good for a man not to touch a woman in this kind of ceremony. He is not saying not to marry, but that they are not to go outside the bonds of marriage:

Nevertheless, because of sexual immorality, let each man have his own wife, and let each woman have her own husband. (verse 2)

The word for *own* here has a beautiful meaning: "her very own" and "his very own." How meaningful that is today, when a wife knows she has the undivided love of her husband and the husband knows he has the exclusive love of his wife.

Now Paul goes on to say in verse 3,

Let the husband render to his wife the affection due her, and likewise also the wife to her husband.

I would like to deal with these subjects in greater detail, but let me just add that to render *affection* or *benevolence*, as some have translated it, literally means to pay a debt.

In other words, Paul is saying that sex for the believer is to be within the framework of marriage only. And let that be said to believers today. We are living in a loose, immoral age in which premarital and extramarital sex is being encouraged and glorified. But for the believer, God warns there is tragedy ahead if you move outside His framework. Many of us who do counseling can tell you that there are a lot of wrecked lives along the highway of life today because men and women have violated God's clear instructions. Oh, my friend, don't think you can beat God in this game and get by with it!

CHAPTER 3

WHY DO CHRISTIAN MARRIAGES FAIL?

As we come to this subject, let me say again that about 75 percent of Christian marriages that fail are the fault of the man. The husband is the one who should have taken the lead. A man must love his wife first, and many men just don't seem to understand what love is. It is an emotion that involves the mind, the will, and it involves the entire being of man. Actually, sex is only one expression of it. Robert Browning put it like this:

God be thanked, the meanest of His creatures
Boasts two soul-sides, one to face the world with,
One to show a woman when he loves her.[1]

Love on Demand

No man has a right to *demand* love of his wife— he must show love and gentleness and kindness. In the early stages of marriage when the marital troubles erupt, the man can save the marriage. But if he does not, the couple will pass the place of no return.

The man is in the driver's seat during the honeymoon. If she loved him enough to marry him, she loves him enough now to follow him. She was made to respond to him, and she will, if he leads in a Spirit-filled manner. Wives have said to me when the question has come up in counseling, "I knew I had made a mistake on my honeymoon." When I hear that, I feel like weeping. It is the most tragic thing that can happen.

Marriage Is Not for Boys

Some men are not prepared for marriage, and I'm convinced of that. I have now come to the position that I will not marry a teenage boy to anyone. A teenage boy is not prepared to assume the responsibility and take the lead in marriage. And until he is prepared, my beloved, that marriage is bound to come to some sort of tragedy later on.

Women to Watch Out For

Now I know that there are some folks who are saying, "Aren't women to blame at all? You are giving the men a rough time here." All right, men, you can relax—I am through with you for a while.

There are certain women who can never become good wives. They will never be able to answer, never be able to agree to any man.

Number one is the dominant female. Let's call her Dominant Delilah. That's the woman who runs every aspect of her home *and* her husband. When she does, she's entirely out of character. I do not believe most women want to take the lead, so what is it that causes this domination? Well, she may have a higher IQ than her husband, or she may have a stronger personality. As a result, he may become a little Mr. Milquetoast. I feel sorry when such a marriage takes place today. She becomes frustrated and begins to nag and criticize her husband and find fault with him.

Two girls who had been together in college met years later on the street. One said to the other, "Are you married?"

"Yes."

"Forgive me for laughing, but I remember that when we were in college you used to say you wouldn't marry the most perfect man on earth."

Her curt reply was, "I didn't!"

Some men marry women who are headstrong and competitors with their men. When a woman does this, she loses her femininity. Sometimes after she rules the roost at home, she looks for other worlds to conquer. She becomes involved in clubs—these are the club women we see today. Some even get involved in politics. Others become unusually good businesswomen and launch a career of their own. This is not meant to imply that all career women are Dominant Delilahs. Sometimes they come over to the church and try to run the preacher. That's when we preachers have fun.

I remember it was said of Dr. Jim McGinley that when one of these Dominant Delilahs said to him in disgust, "If you were my husband, I'd poison your coffee," his instant reply was, "If you were my wife, I'd drink it!" The dominant female is never prepared to be a real wife.

The second woman is one who is ruled by envy and jealousy. You'll always find that these women are the gossips. So let's call her Gossipy Gussie. I have never yet seen a gossip who had a happy home. These are the frigid women of today. The husband and the children are miserable, and she is incapable of answering or agreeing as a wife. Every church has a few of these. They wreck their own homes, and they attempt to wreck their churches.

The third one is the neurotic woman. Let's call her Hysterical Hortense, or if she's not too extreme, we could call her Nervous Nellie. When she doesn't get her way, she's the one who acts up. Her husband always walks on eggshells. He wasn't quite what she thought he was, and she begins to make him over. I heard of a husband who asked his wife one day, "Why in the world did you ever marry me when you found out there were so many things wrong with me?" She wanted to make him over altogether. What if he doesn't fall into her pattern? She'll give him the silent treatment and pout for days. There will be a tense atmosphere in the home.

This woman, of course, is never prepared for marriage at all.

Then there is the woman who marries so that she might have financial security. We'll call her Gold-Digger Gertie, and unfortunately, there are Christians today who are like that. May I say this to you, dear ladies, if you are looking for the type of man who can take care of you financially, you may have peace and security regarding the finances, but you will never know what real love is, nor the peace and joy of being able to agree with a husband who really loves you.

When Marriage Fails

When you have a failed marriage, what can you do? There are three scriptural procedures that could be followed.

Bear it. You can grit your teeth and clench your fists and continue on and bear it. You can maintain a front that all is well, and there are many Christians today who are following this line. Some of them, I think, are doing it for worthy reasons—for the sake of the children, for the sake of their testimony—and they will continue to walk together through life, although it becomes almost unbearable at times.

Separate. The second way is separation but not divorce. One leaves the other, desertion maybe, or because of certain things in the home.

Friend, there are many things that can happen even in a Christian home that will cause the wife to have to separate from her husband or vice versa. Now marital difficulties are rough, sometimes like the eruption of Mount Vesuvius, and I do not believe that God has ever asked any man or woman to stay in a "living hell" down here. But that means only separation.

Divorce. The third action, of course, is divorce. Let's be very clear today, this is where it gets complicated. But as far as Scripture is concerned, divorce is permitted for specific reasons and in some cases remarriage is allowed.

Civil divorce, the kind of divorce they grant at the courthouse, and scriptural divorce are not always the same thing—in fact, in most cases they are not. Therefore we as pastors have a very difficult situation. There are times when a man or woman must get a civil divorce to protect themselves or the children. In one marriage I counseled, the husband was a compulsive gambler, and he had gambled away one million dollars. They had children, and she needed to protect those children. But I made it very clear to her that even though she got a divorce, in God's sight that would not give her permission to remarry. So we must recognize that our civil laws today are way out of kilter as far as the Word of God is concerned. There is more detail on this matter of divorce in Chapter 7.

What Did Jesus Say?

Now I want to focus on what our Lord said on this subject. And if you think I am out of line, will you listen to Him in Matthew 19—my Lord did not mind dealing with this sensitive issue.

The Pharisees also came to Him, testing Him, and saying to Him, "Is it lawful for a man to divorce his wife for just any reason?" And He answered and said to them, "Have you not read that He who made them at the beginning 'made them male and female' . . . ?" (Matthew 19:3–4)

Our Lord goes back to the original creation. God's ideal is one man and one woman. This is not just romantic. Oh, young person, wait for the one God has for you to come along. God will show you. Don't jump into your first opportunity for marriage. Oh, the tragedies of that today! And couples come to us for counseling too late.

"'For this reason a man shall leave his father and mother and be joined to his wife, and the two shall become one flesh'? So then, they are no longer two but one flesh. Therefore what God has joined together, let not man separate." They said to Him, "Why then did Moses command to give a certificate of divorce, and to put her away?" (Matthew 19:5–7)

Now our Lord has stated God's ideal, that if you get the one person God has for you, these matters of separation and divorce and marital problems will probably never be yours. But we live in a world of sin, and there are a lot of young people getting the wrong advice today, and there are a lot of wrong marriages being made today. Our Lord continued:

He said to them, "Moses, because of the hardness of your hearts, permitted you to divorce your wives, but from the beginning it was not so. And I say to you, whoever divorces his wife, except for sexual immorality, and marries another, commits adultery; and whoever marries her who is divorced commits adultery." (Matthew 19:8–9)

Our Lord made it very clear that He gave one ground for divorce, and that is unfaithfulness to the marriage vow. Why did Moses permit the writing of a bill of divorcement? Again our Lord made it clear, "because of the hardness of your hearts."

Husbands, love your wives; wives, answer to them, agree to them. My friend, you cannot emotionally, verbally, or physically brutalize a woman all day and then expect her to show love and affection at night. How many men today have made a tragedy of their marriages because they brutalized the love of a woman! God has permitted divorce because of the hardness of your hearts.

My friend, don't miss this: "Husbands, love your wives, just as Christ also loved the church and gave Himself for her" (Ephesians 5:25).

CHAPTER 4

SEX IN MARRIAGE

Marriage, or more specifically the important role of sex within marriage, is the theme of this chapter. I think we will be handling it in a more dignified manner than is usual today because we are going to follow the counsel of the apostle Paul to the Corinthians as he guided those new believers in their Christian lives.

Previously Paul had given them the spiritual truths that, by application to the problems encountered in marriage, can solve matters relating to sex in marriage. He had emphasized that our bodies belong to God, and that a Christian's body is the temple of the Holy Spirit and is to be used for the glory of God.

To Marry or Not to Marry?

Now concerning the things of which you wrote to me: It is good for a man not to touch a woman. (1 Corinthians 7:1)

It is obvious that the Corinthian believers had written a letter to Paul concerning this problem. We do not have their question, but we do have Paul's answer. Paul took a long time getting to his answer because he first felt it necessary to deal with the divisions and the scandals in their midst. However, he had no reluctance in dealing with the subject of marriage and he writes boldly and very frankly. Before we get into the text itself, let me deal with two introductory matters.

First there is the question: Was Paul ever married? If Paul was never married, then in his explanation he is simply theorizing and not speaking from experience. However, Paul did not do that; he always spoke from experience. It was not the method of the Spirit of God to choose a man who knew nothing about the subject on which the Spirit of God wanted him to write.

It has generally been assumed—judging from verse 7—that Paul was not married:

For I wish that all men were even as I myself. But each one has his own gift from God, one in this manner and another in that.

If we are going to assume that Paul was not married, we need to pay attention to the verse that follows:

But I say to the unmarried and to the widows: It is good for them if they remain even as I am. (1 Corinthians 7:8)

Someone will say, "He still says he is unmarried." Granted, we know he was not married at the time of his writing, but notice that he mentions two classes here: the unmarried and the widows or widowers. The Greek word *chera* includes both widows and widowers. He could have never married, or he could have been a widower.

It is difficult to believe that Paul had always been unmarried because of his background and because he was a member of the Sanhedrin. In Acts 26:10 Paul says, "This I also did in Jerusalem, and many of the saints I shut up in prison, having received authority from the chief priests; and when they were put to death, I cast my vote against them." How could he cast his vote against them? He could not have done so unless he was a member of the Sanhedrin.

So since Paul *was* a member of the Sanhedrin, he must have been a married man because that was one of the conditions of membership. There was an insistence upon Jewish young men to marry. The Mishna said this should be at the age of eighteen. In the *Yebhamoth*, the commentary on Genesis 5:2 states: "A Jew who has no wife is not a man." I believe it is an inescapable conclusion that Paul at one time was a married man. He undoubtedly was a widower who had not remarried. In 1 Corinthians 9:5 we read,

Do we have no right to take along a believing wife, as do also the other apostles, the brothers of the Lord, and Cephas?

I think Paul is saying, "I could marry again if I wanted to—there would be no objection to that but

I won't do it for the simple reason that I would not ask a woman to follow me around in the type of ministry God has given me."

In the classic work of F. W. Farrar, the *Life and Work of St. Paul*, he deals with this question: Was Saul married? "Had he the support of some loving heart during the fiery struggles of his youth? Amid the to-and-fro contentions of spirit which resulted from an imperfect and unsatisfying creed, was there in the troubled sea of his life one little island home where he could find refuge from incessant thoughts? Little as we know of his domestic relations, little as he cared to mingle mere private interests with the great spiritual truths which occupy his soul, it seems to me that we must answer this question in the affirmative."[1]

The position of many expositors is that Paul had been married and that his wife had died. Paul never made reference to her, but he spoke so tenderly of the marriage relationship in Ephesians 5 that I believe he had been married to some good woman who reciprocated his love.

The Situation in Corinth

The second introductory matter is not a question but a statement. We need to understand the Corinth of that day. If we do not, we are going to fall into the trap of saying that Paul was commending the single state above the married state. One must understand the local situation of Corinth to know

what he was talking about. Notice the first two
verses again:

**Now concerning the things of which you wrote
to me: It is good for a man not to touch a
woman. Nevertheless, because of sexual
immorality, let each man have his own wife,
and let each woman have her own husband.**

We need to understand Corinth. I've mentioned
this before but it bears repeating. I have been to
the ruins of ancient Corinth and have seen above
those ruins the mountain that was the acropolis,
called Acro-Corinthus. The city was dominated by
the Acro-Corinthus, and on top of it was the temple of Aphrodite. It towered over the city like a dark
cloud. Today the ruins of a Crusader fort are there.
When the Crusaders came, they used the stones
from the temple of Aphrodite to build their fortress.

This temple was like most heathen temples: sex
was a religion. There were one thousand so-called
vestal virgins there. In that temple you could get
food, drink, and sex. Those vestal virgins were nothing in the world but one thousand prostitutes and
sex was carried on in the name of religion. That
was the philosophy of Plato, by the way.

People tend to forget the immorality of that culture. A man once said to me, "Socrates wrote in a
very lofty language." Yes, sometimes he did. He also
told prostitutes how they ought to conduct themselves. The whole thought was to get rid of the
desires of the body. The effort to do that came out
in two major philosophies of the Greeks: Stoicism

said the basic desires were to be denied; Epicure-anism said basic desires were to be satisfied and fulfilled all the way, which is hedonism.

The wife in the Roman world was mere chattel; she was a workhorse. A man generally had several wives. One had charge of the kitchen, another had charge of the living area, another was in charge of the clothes. You will find the same thing among the Bedouins in Palestine today. They have several wives, and it is a practical thing for them. One takes care of the sheep, another goes with the man as he wanders around, another stays back at the home base where they probably have a few fruit trees. He thinks he needs at least three wives.

But getting back to Corinth, in an unsaved man's relationship with his wife (or wives), sex was secondary because the man went up to the temple where the good-looking girls were kept. There they celebrated the seasons of fertility, and believe me, friend, that is what was carried on.

Now Paul was lifting marriage up to the heights, out of that degradation, and he said to the Corinthian believers, "Don't live like that." Every man was to have one wife, and every woman was to have her own husband. Christianity lifted woman from the place of slavery in the pagan world of the Roman Empire and made her a companion of man, restoring her to her rightful position. Paul was in Ephesus when he wrote to the Corinthians, and located in Ephesus was the awful temple of Diana. It was to the Ephesians that Paul wrote, "Husbands, love your wives, just as Christ also loved the church and gave Himself for her."

Paul lifts woman from slave status to that of a partner of man. Look at two verses:

Let the husband render to his wife the affection due her, and likewise also the wife to her husband.

She is to respond to him. He is to tell her that he loves her.

The wife does not have authority over her own body, but the husband does. And likewise the husband does not have authority over his own body, but the wife does. (1 Corinthians 7:3–4)

The man is not to run up to that temple of Aphrodite. Love and sex are to take place at home. That is exactly what Paul is saying here. And Hebrews 13:4 reinforces this:

Marriage is honorable among all, and the bed undefiled; but fornicators and adulterers God will judge.

"Marriage is honorable among all." Young man, if you find a Christian girl who will have you, get married. Young lady, if you find a Christian fellow who will have you, get married. I believe that God will lead you to the right one, if you are willing to be led in that way.

Marriage is honorable among all, and sex is to be exercised within the framework of marriage. God gave marriage to mankind for the *welfare* of the human family. I know I sound like a square, because this idea of living together without being married has become very commonplace, but I must tell you, young or not-so-young person, that you will surely pay for it if you attempt to live together outside the bonds of marriage. The home is the very center of the whole social structure, and it is the very center of the church.

"And the bed undefiled." That is, let the marriage bed be kept undefiled. There is nothing wrong with sex—except it is being taught too much in our schools, as well as by practically every other means of communication in our society today. The result is promiscuity, which is responsible for an epidemic of horrible venereal diseases including HIV, the deadly AIDS virus.

"But fornicators and adulterers God will judge." This statement leads me to repeat with emphasis Galatians 6:7: "Do not be deceived, God is not mocked; for whatever a man sows, that he will also reap." This is very severe, but after years in the ministry, I have watched many Christians who have tried to get by with sexual sins, and I do not know of any who have been able to do it. Maybe they have not been detected, but they have not gotten by with it as far as God is concerned. He has judged them!

Again, "marriage is honorable among all," the only motive for marriage is love—not sex, but love. I am convinced that Paul had known the love of a good and great woman. So many of the great men in Scripture knew the love of a wonderful wife.

Why Marry?

Now Paul continues his guidelines for conduct in marriage.

Do not deprive one another except with consent for a time, that you may give yourselves to fasting and prayer; and come together again so that Satan does not tempt you because of your lack of self control. But I say this as a concession, not as a commandment. (1 Corinthians 7:5–6)

Although Paul's counsel is not a commandment, it is a good guideline to follow so that Satan will not have an opportunity to tempt either member of the marriage relationship.

For I wish that all men were even as I myself. But each one has his own gift from God, one in this manner and another in that. (1 Corinthians 7:7)

At this time Paul did not have a wife and did not remarry. He was not taking a wife along with him on his travels. Like Paul, there have been people in the Lord's work through the centuries who have not married. They have made that kind of sacrifice—some for several years, some for their whole lifetime. You remember that the Lord Jesus said,

> **For there are eunuchs who were born thus from their mother's womb, and there are eunuchs who were made eunuchs by men, and there are eunuchs who have made themselves eunuchs for the kingdom of heaven's sake . . .** (Matthew 19:12)

When I began in the ministry, I attempted to imitate a pastor who was a bachelor. I thought that was the happiest state, but I soon learned it wasn't for me. I wanted a wife. Paul says that is all right—"Each one has his own gift from God."

> **But I say to the unmarried and to the widows: It is good for them if they remain even as I am; but if they cannot exercise self-control, let them marry. For it is better to marry than to burn with passion.** (1 Corinthians 7:8–9)

Why Stay Married?

> **Now to the married I command, yet not I but the Lord: A wife is not to depart from her husband. But even if she does depart, let her remain unmarried or be reconciled to her husband. And a husband is not to divorce his wife.** (7:10–11)

Here is a commandment. Paul is putting it on the line. The wife is not to leave her husband, and the husband is not to leave his wife. If one or the other is going to leave, then they should remain unmarried.

Now there was the problem that presented itself in Corinth. After Paul had come and preached the gospel to them, a husband in a family would accept Christ but the wife would not. In another family it might be that the wife would accept Christ and the husband would not. What were the believers to do under such circumstances?

> **But to the rest I, not the Lord, say: If any brother has a wife who does not believe, and she is willing to live with him, let him not divorce her. And a woman who has a husband who does not believe, if he is willing to live with her, let her not divorce him. For the unbelieving husband is sanctified by the wife, and the unbelieving wife is sanctified by the husband; otherwise your children would be unclean, but now they are holy.** (1 Corinthians 7:12–14)

If one was married to an unsaved spouse, and there were children in the family, Paul said they should try to see it through. Paul said, "Stay right where you are if you can."

> **But if the unbeliever departs, let him depart; a brother or a sister is not under bondage in such cases. But God has called us to peace.** (1 Corinthians 7:15)

If the unbeliever walks out of the marriage, that is another story. Then the believer is free.

Now the next question that is asked is whether that one is free to marry again. I believe that under certain circumstances Paul would have given permission for it. I do not think one can put down a categorical rule either way for today. I think that each case stands or falls on its own merits. Unfortunately this can easily be abused, even by Christians. I am afraid sometimes a husband or a wife tries to get rid of the other and forces them to leave in order that they might have "scriptural ground" for divorce.

For how do you know, O wife, whether you will save your husband? Or how do you know, O husband, whether you will save your wife? (1 Corinthians 7:16)

This should be the goal of the Christian wife. I know several women who were married to unsaved men and tried to win them for Christ. This also should be the goal of the husband who is married to an unsaved woman. Winning them for Christ should be uppermost in their consideration.

But as God has distributed to each one, as the Lord has called each one, so let him walk. And so I ordain in all the churches. (1 Corinthians 7:17)

Paul was advising people to stay where they were. They were not to walk out of their marriage after they had heard and accepted the gospel. They were to stay married if their unbelieving partner would allow it.

> **Were you called while a slave? Do not be concerned about it; but if you can be made free, rather use it. For he who is called in the Lord while a slave is the Lord's freedman. Likewise he who is called while free is Christ's slave.** (1 Corinthians 7:21–22)

I find today that there are many homemakers who feel pressured to have an outside career and they become so involved in it that they neglect their families.

> **You were bought at a price; do not become slaves of men.** (1 Corinthians 7:23)

You have been redeemed by the blood of Jesus Christ. Now don't be a slave to someone else. Does this sound like a contradiction? Let me explain by an example. A cocktail waitress was converted by hearing the gospel on our radio broadcast. Everything about the Bible was brand-new to her. She asked me a question about whether she should give up being a cocktail waitress because she just didn't feel right about it anymore. I answered that it was up to her. I said, "That is a decision you must make. If you have a conviction about it, then give it up. If you want to know what I think about it personally, I think you ought to give it up. However, don't give it up because I say so, but give it up if that becomes your conviction." She did give it up and found another job within a couple of weeks. She had been bought with a price; she was not to be a servant of man.

Brethren, let each one remain with God in that state in which he was called. (1 Corinthians 7:24)

This is the important consideration. When we are converted, whatever we are doing, wherever we are, we're to remain in that position as long as we are free in our relationship to God. God must be first in our lives. "Remain with God in that state." If our situation will not permit God to be first, then we should change the situation, as the cocktail waitress did.

A Word to Singles

The discussion for the remainder of 1 Corinthians 7 is an answer to the second question that the people had asked Paul and is related to the first question. Remember that all this must be interpreted in the light of what Corinth was in Paul's day, and then it can be applied to the day in which we live. Corinth was such a corrupt place, and manhood was corrupted there. When womanhood is corrupted, manhood will descend to a low level—that has always been the story. So there was this question among Christian parents in Corinth: What should they do about their marriageable daughters? Before they were converted, their friends were drunken sots who went up to the temple of Aphrodite to the prostitutes there. What should the single Christian girls do now? Paul dealt with this question.

> **Now concerning virgins: I have no commandment from the Lord; yet I give judgment as one whom the Lord in His mercy has made trustworthy.** (1 Corinthians 7:25)

"Now concerning virgins"—several of the translations have it: "Now concerning virgin *daughters*," which I think clarifies it. That is really what Paul was talking about here.

This reveals that Paul knew the commandments of the Lord Jesus Christ and what He taught. However, he specifically said here that concerning virgins he had no commandment of the Lord. "But," he said, "I give my own judgment." He was giving his opinion as a capable judge because he had obtained the mercy of God, and he wanted to be faithful to God. In other words, he possessed the qualifications a judge should have, as he had told them in chapter 6.

> **I suppose therefore that this is good because of the present distress—that it is good for a man to remain as he is: Are you bound to a wife? Do not seek to be loosed. Are you loosed from a wife? Do not seek a wife.** (1 Corinthians 7:26–27)

"The present distress" was that awful situation in Corinth, which Paul knew was not going to continue.

Someone asked me, "Do you think this excessive immorality and this lawlessness in our nation will continue?" If it does continue, my friend, it will bring down our houses and destroy our nation—then it will be ended for sure.

Now what was Paul saying? My paraphrase: "In the present distress, since you have come to Christ at such a difficult time, if you are bound to a wife, stay with her. If she is unsaved, stay with her as long as you can. However, if you are not married, then, because of the present distress with the tremendous immorality that is here, it would be best for you to remain single." Paul says this is his judgment.

But even if you do marry, you have not sinned; and if a virgin marries, she has not sinned. Nevertheless such will have trouble in the flesh, but I would spare you. (1 Corinthians 7:28)

Of course it is not sinful to marry. But the sea of matrimony is rough, even under the most favorable circumstances. He is trying to save them from much trouble. That reminds me of the country boy who was being married. The preacher said to him, "Wilt thou have this woman to be thy lawfully wedded wife?" The young fellow answered, "I wilt." And I guess he did!

In our day we are seeing the shipwreck of a growing number of marriages among both Christians and non-Christians. This reveals that we also have a "present distress."

Married or Single—Put God First

Now Paul goes on to discuss other things with them, all in the light of the present distress, the shortness of time, the urgency and immediacy of the hour.

Marriage is the first topic he discussed. "Sure," Paul said in effect, "it is all right to go ahead and marry, but remember that you will have trouble." And they would! In counseling I have tried to tell young people that the romantic period will pass. When the first month's rent comes due and there is not much money in the treasury, believe me, romance flies out the window.

> **But this I say, brethren, the time is short, so that from now on even those who have wives should be as though they had none.** (1 Corinthians 7:29)

Paul is saying that in spite of the stress of the times, they are to put God first. If you are married, can you act as if you are not married, in that you put God first?

> **Those who weep as though they did not weep, those who rejoice as though they did not rejoice, those who buy as though they did not possess.** (1 Corinthians 7:30)

"Those who weep as though they did not weep." Are you going to let some sorrow, some tragedy in your life, keep you from serving God?

"Those who rejoice as though they did not rejoice." Are you going to let pleasure take the place of your relationship to God, as many do?

"Those who buy as though they did not possess." Will you let your business take the place of God? Many a man has made business his god.

> **And those who use this world as not misusing it. For the form of this world is passing away.** (1 Corinthians 7:31)

"The form of this world is passing away." Do the things of this life control you, or does Christ control your life? This is what Paul is talking about.

Now Paul goes back to a discussion of marriage.

> **But I want you to be without care. He who is unmarried cares for the things of the Lord— how he may please the Lord.** (1 Corinthians 7:32)

Paul then gives some practical observations. The unmarried person doesn't have to worry about changing the baby's diapers or going out to buy food for the family but can give more time to the things of God.

> **But he who is married cares about the things of the world—how he may please his wife.** (1 Corinthians 7:33)

The married man tries to please his wife. This is normal and natural, and Paul is not saying it is wrong.

There is a difference between a wife and a virgin. The unmarried woman cares about the things of the Lord, that she may be holy both in body and in spirit. But she who is married cares about the things of the world—how she may please her husband. And this I say for your own profit, not that I may put a leash on you, but for what is proper, and that you may serve the Lord without distraction. (1 Corinthians 7:34–35)

Paul is making it very clear that the important thing is to put God first. That should be the determining factor for every person in a marriage relationship. I don't care who you are or how spiritual you think you may be, if you are not putting God first in your marriage, then your marriage, my friend, is not the Christian marriage God intends it to be.

He comes back to his judgment that the single person can attend upon the Lord without distraction.

A wife is bound by law as long as her husband lives; but if her husband dies, she is at liberty to be married to whom she wishes, only in the Lord. (1 Corinthians 7:39)

That is, she is to marry another Christian, of course.

But she is happier if she remains as she is, according to my judgment—and I think I also have the Spirit of God. (7:40)

Paul makes it clear again that this is his judgment, his advice. The important thing is to serve God, to put God first in your life. If a person is married, God should still be first in his life. Unfortunately, there are many Christian couples who are compatible—they are not going to the divorce court—but God does not have first place in their marriage.

In deciding your marital status, the most important consideration is not what your Christian friends will say or how society in general will regard you. The question you need to ask yourself is: In what way can I put God first in my life?

CHAPTER 5

THE BEST LOVE

I must put down at the beginning a rather black background, and I trust the picture we shall place on this background will be rewarding enough to justify the introduction.

There is an obsession with sex today that is positively frightening and absolutely alarming! You need only to consult contemporary literature to recognize this. In a leading British paper not long ago this statement was made: "Popular morality is now a wasteland, littered with the debris of broken convictions." And it was a judge of the Superior Court of Massachusetts who said, "At too many colleges today, sexual promiscuity among students is a dangerous and growing evil." The Billy Graham paper, *Decision*, carried an editorial on the church and the moral crisis. In it there was this quotation: "So our young people go riding down the high road to hell in an atmosphere that would make any self-respecting animal sick to its stomach, and no one thinks that matters are as bad as they seem." An outstanding Christian writer in America says:

But where are the compelling external cries to match the inner voices of the soul which at times murmur darkly and other times shout clamorously that all is not well, that wayward feet are treading the way of wrath, the path of judgment? The answer is not simply in passing more laws. It is to be found in regeneration by His Spirit, who alone can set men's souls on fire with a divinely sent thirst for greater purity, both for the individual and for the body politic. Apart from such spiritual burning and purging, men sink beneath the weight and corruption of their own sin.

There are other voices being lifted in alarm. But all about us are the advocates of this erotic cult who falsely claims that all of this emphasis on sex is a signal of a new, broad-minded and enlightened era. The facts reveal that there is nothing new about it. Furthermore it does not mark the entrance to abundant living. On the contrary, it has characterized the demise of all decadent and decaying civilizations—Egypt, Babylon, Greece, and Rome—to name but a few. The sex symbol marks the decline and fall of many a great and noble people; it is part of the death rattle of a fading nation. The French Revolution marked the departure of the glory of France, and it was during that time that a prostitute was placed on an altar and worshiped.

The excuse for paying this abnormal attention to the subject, given by these purveyors of filth and licentiousness, is that a bluenosed generation of the past put the lid down on it. The false charge is made that the Bible and the church have frowned upon the subject of sex until it is taboo today and can only be whispered in secret. They go on to place the blame of present-day marriage failures and the increase in divorce on the gross ignorance of young people. "If only they knew more about this fascinating subject," they counsel, "there would be success in marriage." Also they play upon the fact that we Americans do not like censorship, and therefore even the basest element in society should be free to say and publish what they choose.

Well, these modern pied pipers of Hamelin are leading the younger generation into a moral morass of debauchery with dirty films and pornographic literature. They give the impression that you must be knowledgeable of this lascivious and salacious propaganda to be sophisticated and suave and sharp. These filthy dreamers have flooded the marketplace and the schoolroom today with this smut and depravity—so much so that a modern father said, "It is not how much shall I tell my son, but how much does he know that I don't know!" In spite of all this new emphasis on sex, the divorce courts continue to grind out their monotonous story of the tragedy of modern marriage in ever-increasing numbers.

Now a knowledge of the physical may have its place in preparation for a happy marriage, but it is inadequate *per se* to make a happy home, and it gives a perverted and abnormal emphasis that does not belong there. Someone once said, "One of the troubles with the world is that people mistake sex for love, money for brains, and transistor radios for civilization." That is the problem of the hour.

The Word of God treats the subject of sex with boldness, frankness, and directness. It is not handled as a dirty subject, and it is not taboo nor theoretical, but it is plain and theological. The Bible is straightforward, and it deals with it in high and lofty language. I think it is time that God is heard. I feel that the pulpit is long overdue in presenting what God has to say on this subject.

In the very beginning it was God who created them male and female. It was *God* who brought the woman to the man. And I would like to add this, He did not need to give Adam a lecture on the birds and bees. God blessed them, and marriage became sacred and holy and pure. And, my friend, it is the only relationship among men and women that God does bless down here—He promises to bless no other. He says that if marriage is made according to His plan, He will bless it down here. (See Genesis 1:27 and Matthew 19:4–6.)

God wants His children to be happily married. He has a plan and purpose for every one of us if we would only listen to Him. The Lord Jesus says to the church at Ephesus:

Nevertheless I have this against you, that you have left your first love. (Revelation 2:4)

Yet the church in Ephesus is the church at its best. It has never been on a higher spiritual level since then. It is difficult for us in this cold day of apostasy to conceive of the lofty plane to which the Holy Spirit had brought the early church in its personal relationship to Christ. The believers in the early church were *in love* with Christ. They loved Him! And five million in the early centuries of Christianity sealed that love with their own blood by dying as martyrs for Him.

I would like to make a change in the translation of Revelation 2:4. The word for "first love" is *protan* in the Greek. It actually means the "best." It is the same word our Lord used in the parable of the prodigal son, in which the father put on the son the *protan* robe—the first, the foremost, the "best" robe, if you please. To the Ephesian believers, Christ is talking about the *best* love. To this church on its high plane, into which a coolness was creeping, Christ says, "Nevertheless I have against you that you are leaving [they had not yet left] your best love." Salvation is a love affair. The question that the Lord asks all of us is, "Do you love Me?" He is not asking, "Are you going to be faithful?" He is not asking, "How much are you going to give, or how much are you going to do?" He is saying, "Do you love Me?" The apostle John put it like this: "We love Him because He first loved us" (1 John 4:19).

The second book I ever wrote was on the little Book of Ruth. My reason for writing it was to show that redemption is a romance. God took the lives of two ordinary people, a very strong and virile man and a very beautiful and noble woman, and He told their love story. In the story God revealed to man

His great love for him. It was a way to get this amazing fact through to us. Salvation is a love affair.

In Christ's last letter to the Ephesian church here in Revelation, He sounds a warning. We do not quite understand this. But I go back thirty or forty years to His first letter to these believers, written through Paul. We call it the Epistle of Paul to the Ephesians. In this epistle He discussed this matter of marital love and compared it to the love of Christ for the church. This has been one of the most misunderstood passages in the Word of God. Listen:

> **Wives, submit to your own husbands, as to the Lord.** (Ephesians 5:22)

There has been natural resentment against this on the part of some, especially very dominant women, for many years. But to resent this is to miss the meaning that is here. Submission is actually for the purpose of headship in the home. It is not a question of one lording it over the other. It is headship for the purpose of bringing order into the home. In addition to this it reveals something else that is quite wonderful. He said,

> **For the husband is head of the wife, as also Christ is head of the church; and He is the Savior of the body.** (Ephesians 5:23)

The analogy, you see, is to Christ and the church. Christian marriage down here, if it is made under the Lord, is a miniature of the relationship of Christ and the church. Christian marriage is an adumbration of that wonderful relationship between Christ and the believer. Christian marriage and the relationship of Christ and the church are sacred.

Now will you listen to me very carefully. The physical act of marriage is sacred. It is a religious ritual; it is a sacrament. I do not mean a sacrament made by a church, nor is it made by a man-made ceremony. But it is a sacrament that is made by God Himself, one which He sanctifies, and He says that this relationship is to reveal to you the love of Christ for your soul. Therefore the woman is to see in a man one to whom she can yield herself in a glorious abandonment. She can give herself wholly and completely and find perfect fulfillment and satisfaction in this man, because this is the man for her.

Spurgeon had something to say about this. Will you hear him:

She delights in her husband, in his person, his character, his affection; to her he is not only the chief and foremost of mankind, but in her eyes he is all in all. Her heart's love belongs to him, and to him only. He is her little world, her Paradise, her choice treasure. She is glad to sink her individuality in his. She seeks no renown for herself; his honor is reflected upon her, and she rejoices in it. She will defend his name with her dying breath; safe enough is he where she can speak of him. His smiling gratitude is all the reward she seeks. Even in her dress she thinks of him and considers nothing beautiful which is distasteful to him. He has many objects in life, some of which she does not quite understand; but she believes in them all, and anything she can do to promote them she delights to perform. . . . Such a wife, as a true spouse, realizes the model marriage relation and sets forth what our oneness with the Lord ought to be.[1]

My beloved, that is a marvelous picture of the wife in a real Christian marriage. The man is to see in the woman one he can worship. Someone says, "Do you mean worship?" I mean exactly that. What does worship mean? You will find that worship is respect that is paid to worth. If you go back and read the old marriage ceremonies, you will find that the bridegroom always said, "I with my body worship you." That is, he sees in her everything that is worthwhile. He must love her so much that he is willing to die for her.

Now the Bible is very expressive, and I do not know why we should be so reluctant to speak as plainly. If you turn back to the Song of Solomon, you will see the picture of the bridegroom and what he thinks of his bride:

You are all fair, my love,
And there is no spot in you.

Like a lily among thorns,
So is my love among the daughters.
(Song of Solomon 4:7; 2:2)

That is rather expressive, is it not? That is what the bridegroom says. Now hear the words of the bride:

My beloved is mine, and I am his.
He feeds his flock among the lilies.
(Song of Solomon 2:16)

There is no greater compliment!

In that moment of sexual intimacy, intended by God to be of supreme and sweet ecstasy, either the wife will carry him to the skies or plunge him down to the depths of hell. Either the husband will place her on a pedestal and say, "I worship you because I find no spot in you," or else he will treat her with brutality. When the latter happens he will kill her love, and she will hate him and become cold and frigid. In counseling we find that this is one reason that a great many marriages are breaking up.

Bacteriologist Rene Dubois of the Rockefeller Institute has made this statement: "Aimlessness and lack of fulfillment constitute the most common cause of organic and mental disease in the Western world." This lack of fulfillment is breaking up many a marriage. A wife becomes dissatisfied and nagging and the husband settles down to a life of mediocrity. He becomes lonely and either develops into a henpecked milquetoast or a domineering brute. You will find both in our society.

Now let me ask a question: Are you the kind of woman that a man would die for? I am going to be very frank. If you are one of these women who is merely making eyes at every boy that comes along, although you may have beauty and personality, you will never be the kind of woman that a man would die for. If you do not have beauty of character, if you do not have nobility of soul, you will be but a flame without heat, a rainbow without color and a flower without perfume. The Word of God deals with that outward adorning—and do not misunderstand, the Bible does not militate against it. All of us ought to look the best we can. Some of us have our problems, but we should do the best we can with what we have. God intends us to enhance the beauty He has given us. But God puts the emphasis, not on the outward adorning, but on the meek and quiet spirit, the inward adorning that is in God's sight of great value.

> **Do not let your adornment be merely outward—arranging the hair, wearing gold, or putting on fine apparel—rather let it be the hidden person of the heart, with the incorruptible beauty of a gentle and quiet spirit, which is very precious in the sight of God.** (1 Peter 3:3–4)

Now, young man, are you the kind of man that a woman would follow to the ends of the earth? You may look like a model for Hart, Schaffner, and Marx but have no purpose, no ambition, no heart for serving God as a Christian, no capacity for great and deep things, no vision at all. If you are that kind, a woman will not follow you very far. She may go with you down to get the marriage license, but she will also be going down to get the divorce later on.

All across our West there are monuments erected to the pioneer wife and mother. I noticed one the other day as I was traveling through Colorado. She is a fine-looking woman, crowned with a sunbonnet, the children about her. You know she did not go to the psychiatrist or marriage counselor. Do you know why she never had to go to the preacher to talk about her marriage breaking up? Because one day a man came to her and said, "I am going West to build a career and a home. Will you follow me?" She said, "I will." And she learned that this man would stand between her and danger; she had many experiences when he protected her from the menacing Indians. She had no problems about whether he loved her or not and he did not doubt her loyalty. They loved each other. These are the kind of people who built our country. It is the other element that is tearing our lovely country to pieces—how I hate to see it happening!

I know that someone is saying right now, "Preacher, I am not that kind of a person. I'm no hero." Young man, God never said that every girl would fall in love with you. Ninety-nine women may pass you by and see in you only the boy next door. That's all. But let me say to you very seriously, one of these days there will come by a woman who will see in you the knight in shining armor. It is God who gives that highly charged chemistry between a certain man and a certain woman.

A young woman may be saying, "But I'm not beautiful of face or figure." May I say this to you, God never said that you would attract every male—only animals do that. Ninety-nine men will pass you by and see in you no more than what Kipling described, "a rag, a bone, and a hank of hair." But one of these days there will come by a man who will love you if you are the right kind of person. You will become his inspiration. You may inspire him to greatness—to write a book, to compose a masterpiece of poetry or music, to paint a picture, or even to preach a sermon. If you are his inspiration, do not ignore him, do not run from him. God may have placed you together for that very purpose. If in God's plan He intends for you to marry there *will come* that one.

Perhaps you are thinking, "Preacher, you are in the realm of theory. What you are talking about is idealistic. It sounds good in a storybook, but it does not happen in life." You are wrong. It *does* happen.

I think of the story of Matthew Henry. If anyone ever wrote a musty commentary, Matthew Henry did. Although a great work, it is to me the most boring thing I have ever read. I never knew that fellow was romantic at any time in his life. But when he came to London as a young man, he met a very wealthy girl of the nobility. He fell in love with her, and she loved him. Finally, she went to her father to tell him about it. The father, trying to discourage her, said, "That young man has no background. You do not even know where he came from!" She answered, "You are right. I do not know where he came from but *I know where he is going,* and I want to go with him." She went.

I am reminded again of the story of Nathaniel Hawthorne when he lost his job as a clerk. He came home and sank into a chair, discouraged and defeated. His wife came behind him, placed before him pen and paper, and putting her arm about him, said, "Now, Nathaniel, you can do what you always wanted to do, you can write." He wrote *The House of Seven Gables*, *The Scarlet Letter*, and other enduring literature—because a wife was his inspiration. "In one of her last letters the widow of Nathaniel Hawthorne penned this ineradicable hope, which became an anchor of comfort in her soul's sorrow: 'I have an eternity, thank God, in which to know him more and more, or I should die in despair.'"[2]

You say I am talking about theory? I am talking about fact. Consider Adam and Eve. That was a romance.

> **So husbands ought to love their own wives as their own bodies; he who loves his wife loves himself. For no one ever hated his own flesh, but nourishes and cherishes it, just as the Lord does the church. For we are members of His body, of His flesh and of His bones. "For this reason a man shall leave his father and mother and be joined to his wife, and the two shall become one flesh."** (Ephesians 5:28–31)

Eve was created to be a helpmeet for Adam. The language is tremendous. She was taken from his side, not molded from the ground as were the animals, but taken from a part of him so that he actually was incomplete until they were together. God fashioned her into the loveliest thing in His creation, and He brought her to Adam. She was a helpmeet, she compensated for what he lacked, for he was not complete in himself. She was made for him, and they became one.

And Adam said:
"This is now bone of my bones
And flesh of my flesh;
She shall be called Woman,
Because she was taken out of Man."
(Genesis 2:23)

Let me move down in history to the early twelfth century. I want to take up a story that always has thrilled me. It is the true story of Abelard and Heloise. When John Lord wrote his *Great Women*, he used Heloise as the example of marital love. The story concerns a young ecclesiastic by the name of Abelard. He was a brilliant young teacher and preacher at what became the University of Paris. The canon had a niece by the name of Heloise whom he sent to be under Abelard's instruction. She was a remarkable person; he was a remarkable man. You know the story—they fell madly in love. But according to the awful practice of that day—and this day as well—the marriage of a priest was deemed a lasting disgrace. When John Lord wrote their story, he gave this introduction, which I would like to share with you. It is almost too beautiful to read in this day. It is like a dew-drenched breeze blowing from a flower-strewn mountain meadow over the slop bucket and pigsty of our contemporary literature. Here is what he wrote:

When Adam and Eve were expelled from Paradise, they yet found one flower, wherever they wandered, blooming in perpetual beauty. This flower represents a great certitude, without which few would be happy—subtle, mysterious, inexplicable—a great boon recognized alike by poets and moralists, Pagan and Christian; yea, identified not only with happiness, but human existence, and pertaining to the soul in its highest aspirations. Allied with the transient and the mortal, even with the weak and corrupt, it is yet immortal in its nature and lofty in its aims—at once a passion, a sentiment, and an inspiration.

To attempt to describe woman without this element of our complex nature, which constitutes her peculiar fascination, is like trying to act the tragedy of Hamlet without Hamlet himself—an absurdity; a picture without a central figure, a novel without a heroine, a religion without a sacrifice. My subject is not without its difficulties. The passion or sentiment is degrading when perverted, it is exalting when pure. Yet it is not vice I would paint, but virtue; not weakness, but strength; not the transient, but the permanent; not the mortal but the immortal—all that is ennobling in the aspiring soul.[3]

Abelard and Heloise, having fallen in love, were not permitted by the church to marry. Therefore they were married secretly by a friend of Abelard. He continued to teach. But the secret came out when a servant betrayed them, and she was forced into a nunnery. Abelard was probably the boldest thinker the Middle Ages produced. He was among the few who began to preach and teach that the Word of God was man's authority and not the church. This man, a great man, became bitter and sarcastic in his teaching because of what had been denied him. When he was on his deathbed, for he died a great while before Heloise, being twenty years her senior, he asked that she be permitted to come to see him. The church did the cruelest thing of all—they would not allow her to come. Therefore he penned a letter to her. To me it is the most pathetic thing I have ever read. He concludes it with this prayer:

> When it pleased Thee, O Lord, and as it pleased Thee, Thou didst join us, and Thou didst separate us. Now, what Thou hast so mercifully begun, mercifully complete; and after separating us in this world, join us together eternally in heaven.[4]

And I believe in God's heaven they are together.

A recent letter from a bereaved wife reads: "I have just buried my husband, and the preacher told me that we are not to be together in heaven because Christians are neither married nor given in marriage in heaven. But really, it would be very lonesome there and I could not stand it without him." I was able to say to her, "It is true you do not marry nor are given in marriage in heaven—you do that down here. But you will be with him in heaven because you want to be together."

John Wesley's story is not told in England; it is told in this country, in Georgia. When John Wesley came as a young missionary to Georgia, the crown had already sent a nobleman there—I think they wanted to get rid of him at court because he was an insipid fellow, devoid of personality and masculinity. Yet due to the terrible custom of that day, the nobility was entitled to marry the finest, and he had married a woman not only of striking beauty and strong personality, but one who was an outstanding Christian. Then there came into their colony this fiery young missionary. Again you know the story—they fell in love. And that happens to be John Wesley's love story.

He begged her to flee with him and go live among the Indians. She said, "No, John, God has called you to go back to England, and He has called you to do some great service for Him." It was she who sent John Wesley back to England. The night came for his ship to sail. They had to wait for the tide and the wind, and she came down to bid him good-bye. Oh, yes, she held him that night, and he held her, but even the worst critics of Wesley say that nothing took place that was wrong. He still begged her to go with him among the Indians and live. The biographer of Wesley says that he came down that gangplank twice, but she sent him back, back to England—to marry the Methodist Church. He returned to England a brokenhearted man, yet she had become his inspiration.

Back in England he was unhappy and dissatisfied with the legal system he had worked out and by which he was living. He had come to the realization that he was a sinner and was not a converted man. His biographer quoted him as saying,

"I came to America to convert the Indians, but who is going to convert John Wesley?" Several years later he was saved at Aldersgate, and he married a woman who was really a battle-ax. She found out about his romance in America and used to stand up in the service and denounce him. Wesley always felt that it was the judgment of God upon him, and he would just stand there and take it. When she would finish her tirade and sit down, Wesley would stand up to preach, and the Spirit of God would come down upon the congregation. The inspiration for that man was back in Georgia. When she had bidden him good-bye, she said, "Providence and Christ may not let us be together in life, but we shall be together over there."[5]

Oh, I know someone is saying to me, "You have gone back to a romantic period. What about today?" Therefore I want to bring this up to date. Let me bring it down to this generation. I counseled with a Christian man who has permitted me to give part of his story without, of course, betraying any names. He is a very modern man, dedicated to God, wanting God's will in everything. He has met a woman with whom he has fallen in love. A wall separates them. He has described that wall as being as high as heaven and as deep as hell; he will not cross over. I do not know the feelings of the woman. He says she has a warm personality, and to him she is beautiful. He says she is fine and noble and a dedicated Christian and wants God's will in her life. The words that he kept repeating to me were, "She is lovely." She has inspired him, I am sure—and probably she is the only one who can. "But," he says, "we are separated down here."

All right, this generation, go ahead and say it, they are a couple of squares. This generation that has been brainwashed with Freudian psychology says, "Let yourself go. Do what you please, you are to have no inhibitions. Live like animals." No, these folk are not animals. He said that he will wait. With a wry smile, he said this to me, "You know, the walls of Jericho were formidable, but they fell down. If it is God's will, He will remove the wall between us. If not, I remember your sermon on the New Jerusalem, where Christ said, 'Behold, I make all things new.' We have bungled our lives down here, but over there God will let us begin all over again."

I am speaking now to young people. You can have a bargain-basement, secondhand, hand-me-down marriage if you want to. It can be sordid and sorry and shabby. If you take the cheap way, you will have a home that in no respect will represent Christ and the church. It can be a hell down here. Take it from one who has counseled with many couples who are Christians. But, my young person, you can ask God for the best. You can tell Him that you will not accept anything short of the best. And He will give you a life in *living color.*

Sex is not taboo. In a Spirit-filled Christian marriage it is a holy relationship. It is a sacrament, sanctified of God. When it is not, it is no more than an animal act. Sex is not a dirty word; it is a sacred act. It is not salacious; it is sanctified. When a man and a woman give themselves to each other in an act of marital love, they can know the love of Christ as no one else can know it. That is exactly what is said in the Word of God:

This is a great mystery, but I speak concerning Christ and the church. (Ephesians 5:32)

As I have said before, I believe that at one time the apostle Paul was a married man and that he had loved some good woman who returned his love because he spoke so tenderly of the marriage relationship. He wrote: "I cannot quite tell you how wonderful this is, it is a great mystery, but I am really speaking of Christ and the church." Then he comes back and adds,

Nevertheless let each one of you in particular so love his own wife as himself, and let the wife see that she respects her husband. (Ephesians 5:33)

When a man and woman come to that place, then they can know Christ who gave Himself, who gave Himself *in love* for us. And they can know then what it is to bring themselves and offer themselves in total dedication to Him.

Down among the Tzeltal Indians in Mexico there is another love story. It has been put on the screen—you may have seen *The Bill Bentley Story*. Bill Bentley was a fine young missionary among the Tzeltal Indians. He was engaged to a very wealthy, cultured, educated girl in Pennsylvania. She was to come down and marry him. But they never married for Bill

Bentley was struck with an illness and died. Marianna Slocum, the girl to whom he was engaged, said, "I'll go down and finish the job." And she did. She learned that language of those Indians and translated the Word of God for them. Leaving six thousand or more believers behind her, she and a nurse moved on to Colombia in South America to pioneer in one of the Indian tribes that has nothing of the Word of God in their language. Someday she and Bill will have their honeymoon—they never had it down here.

The last time I saw Marianna Slocum was in the airport in Mexico City. She was sitting there praying because we could not get our reservations that Saturday morning, and I had to be here on Sunday. I want to say to you that she *prayed* me on the plane that morning. She has a way with God.

My friend, do you know a Savior who loves you— more than a wife could love you, more than a husband could love you? He has tried every means imaginable to tell you of His love. He gave Himself for you, that He might present you to God without spot, without blemish—which is all His work. He asks of you only that which is asked of any girl when she has a proposal of marriage. She can either say yes or no. You can either say yes or no to Christ who loves you.

And those of us who are His own, may He keep us from leaving the best love. May He sweeten our relationships down here and make our homes truly Christian homes, setting forth the love of our Savior.

CHAPTER 6

WHAT ABOUT MY UNSAVED PARTNER?

In previous chapters we have presented Paul's instructions about marriage to the believers in Ephesus. Now we find that Peter comments on this same theme. Here he speaks of the position of the wife in the home.

> **Wives, likewise, be submissive to your own husbands, that even if some do not obey the word, they, without a word, may be won by the conduct of their wives.** (1 Peter 3:1)

However, Peter is presenting an altogether different situation from that which Paul discussed in Ephesians. Paul dealt with the relationship between a Christian wife and a Christian husband who both were *Spirit-filled* believers. That entire section in Ephesians begins with "be filled with the Spirit" (Ephesians 5:18). When you are filled with the Spirit, what are you to do? Paul says, "Wives, submit to your own husbands, as to the Lord" (Ephesians 5:22), and, "Husbands, love your wives, just as Christ also loved the church and gave Himself for her" (Ephesians 5:25). He is speaking of a Christian home in which both the husband and wife are Spirit-filled believers, and the relationship is one in which the man loves his wife and is willing to die for her.

Now for the sake of order in any situation, there must be headship. In marriage, that headship has been given to the husband. When the wife is told to submit, however, it is not like the obedience of a child. Many men, when they marry, think of their wives as sort of a first child and that she is to obey them as a child is to obey. That is not true at all. As we have suggested before, biblical submission is voluntary. Paul is saying to the wife, "Submit yourself. This man loves you, and you are to submit to him." The better word, because it means more, is *respond*. Respond to this man. If he comes to you as your Christian husband and puts his arms around you and says, "I love you more than anything else," then certainly you should respond, "I love you."

The Marriage Relationship

Down through the years I have counseled a great many young people who have asked me to unite them in marriage. I never tried to marry as many couples as I could. Very frankly, I always did it with fear and trembling. I would like to mention very briefly some things I have told them.

The Physical Plane

Marriage is made on three different planes. The first is the physical plane, and that is important. It is the thing that the world talks about a great deal: the sexual relationship. It is a wonderful thing to have a wife whom you can put your arms around and love. Between two believers, sex can become the most precious, most beautiful, and most wonderful thing there is in this world. It is my conviction that believers are the only ones who can really enjoy the physical relationship to the fullest. There is no question that the physical relationship is wonderful.

Before we got married, my wife felt she was not cut out to be a preacher's wife. She had been brought up in a little town in Texas and had seen how the preacher's wife was expected to do so much work in the church. So I took her to talk with Dr. Lewis Sperry Chafer one day, and I explained her fears to him. Neither of us will ever forget what Dr. Chafer said. He told my wife, "I am out speaking in Bible conferences a great deal. When I come home, I am not looking for the assistant pastor to meet me, nor the organist, nor the president of the missionary society. I want a woman there to meet me who is my wife and whom I can put my arms around and love." The physical relationship is an important part of marriage.

Psychological Relationship

The second plane in marriage is the mental or psychological relationship, which is also very important. On one of our tours to the Bible lands, there was a very wonderful couple who were in their fifties. They would get up early in the morning and take a hike, and again at night they would walk together. They would visit certain places that were not included in the tour. They enjoyed doing things together, and it is wonderful to have that kind of relationship. When a couple's interests and their appetites are altogether different, there isn't that healthy relationship. Because so many husbands and wives do not share the same interests, there are many clubs and lodges today where each can get away from the other and do what they want to do. How tragic that is!

Spiritual Relationship

The third plane in a marriage is the spiritual relationship—and this, of course, applies to a marriage between two believers. When problems and trouble and sorrow and suffering come, a husband and wife should be able to come to God together in prayer and to meet around the Word of God. You can break the other two ties, but "a threefold cord is not quickly broken" (Ecclesiastes 4:12). When you have all three, you have a wonderful marriage. The first two cords can break, but if the third one will hold, the marriage will hold. However, when the third one is broken with the others, the marriage has gone down the tube, my friend. I have to admit there is very little hope for a marriage like that.

We have been discussing marriage between two believers. Suppose, however, that one of them is not a believer. Let's use the wife as our example. Here is a wife married to a man who is not a Christian. To begin with, she should not have married him if she was saved before they married. Any Christian man or woman who marries a non-Christian is in trouble. Scripture forbids marriage between a believer and an unbeliever. In Deuteronomy 22:10 we read, "You shall not plow with an ox and a donkey together." There are a lot of them yoked together today, and it is a big mistake!

One young lady came to me and said, "Dr. McGee, my fiancé is not a believer, but I am going to win him for the Lord."

I said to her, "Have you won him yet?"

"No, he won't come to church with me yet."

So I told her this: "Your greatest influence with that young man is right now. The day you get married, your influence to win him for the Lord will greatly diminish. You'll never be able to preach to him again. You are going to be living with him, and he's going to be watching you very carefully from now on. If you can't get him to church now, you're in trouble."

She did not like what I said. In fact, she went and got another preacher to perform the ceremony because I would not perform it. I have never knowingly married a saved person to an unsaved person because I believe that Scripture teaches it is entirely wrong. Well, she got someone else to marry them, but she came back within two years weeping and wanting to talk to me because she had gotten a divorce from him. Their marriage was headed in that direction even before it started, my friend.

Here in 1 Peter we have that unfortunate relationship in which there is a saved wife and an unsaved husband. Apparently, the wife became a Christian after they had married. Is she to change after her conversion and become a sort of female preacher in the home in order to lecture her husband and to present the gospel to him? No. She is to continue on in the same position, that of being in subjection to him. This means submitting yourself voluntarily. The wife is to continue on in this relationship of voluntary submission, letting her husband—though unsaved—continue to be the head of the house.

Suppose, however, that her husband wants her to go with him to the nightclub and drink cocktails? Is she to do that? I would hope that even these most rabid folk who say that she should obey her husband would agree that she should not do such things. However, there are those who are giving that kind of counsel today.

A lady who attended my church when I was a pastor in downtown Los Angeles had an unsaved husband who wanted her to go to a nightclub, which apparently also had a sort of burlesque show. Some evangelist had counseled her that she was to obey her husband even in this, and so she went. It offended her sensibilities, and she was greatly concerned about it. She actually came to the place where a doctor told her that she would have to enter an institution for psychopathic treatment because she could not go on under that type of pressure. Well, she heard me speaking on the radio, and it was evident that I had a little different idea about it. When she came to talk to me, I told her that I did not believe the Word of God intended for her to do these things. I said that after her conversion she was to try to win her husband and to be subject to him. But I went on to question her. What would she do if her husband wanted her to go out and commit a robbery? Would she have to join him in that and drive the car for him? She said she was sure that the evangelist would not want her to go that far.

May I say to you, her submission was to be voluntary. God certainly did not command her to engage in sinful or questionable activities that would spoil her testimony. A Christian wife must live very carefully before an unsaved husband. Her preaching is not going to do a bit of good. "That . . . they, without a word, may be won by the conduct of their wives." In other words, she is to preach a wordless sermon by her pure life that she lives before him. And that has nothing in the world to do with submission to him.

Peter says that "when they observe your chaste conduct accompanied by fear" (1 Peter 3:2) your husband will recognize that you have now changed and want to live a pure life for God and that you no longer want to indulge in the things of the world.

Therefore, this is the testimony that you can give to him.

Wise Witnessing

Another lady came to me when I was a pastor and said, "Dr. McGee, I bring my husband to church every Sunday." (She was the kind of woman who *could* bring her husband because she had a dominant personality.) She continued, "He is not saved, and every Sunday I think he will make a decision for Christ, but he doesn't. On Monday morning I sit at the breakfast table just weeping and telling him how I wish he would accept Christ. When he comes home from work in the evening, again I just sit there at dinner and weep and beg him to accept Christ."

Well, I got to thinking about what she had said. How would you like to have dinner every evening and breakfast every morning with a weeping woman? I wouldn't care for it myself, and I'm sure you wouldn't want that either. So I called her on the phone and said, "Suppose that for a year's moratorium you simply do not talk to your husband about the Lord at all?" She said, "Oh, you mean that I'm not to witness?" I said, "No, I did not say that. Peter says that if you cannot win your husband with the Word of God, then start preaching a wordless sermon. How about your life? What kind of life are you living before him?" Well, that put her back on her heels because she wasn't living as she knew she should live. But she agreed to my suggestion because she did want to win him, and she was a wonderful woman in many ways. I was amazed myself when, in six months' time, her husband made a decision for Christ one Sunday morning. The wordless sermon had won, my friend.

What About Sex Appeal?

Do not let your adornment be merely outward—arranging the hair, wearing gold, or putting on fine apparel. (1 Peter 3:3)

Obviously, this verse does not prohibit all adorning—if it did, it also would prohibit all apparel!

In the Roman Empire a great emphasis was put upon the way women arranged their hair. If you have seen any pictures of that period, you know that the women loaded their heads down with all kinds of hair—not only their own hair but also someone else's. They really built up their hairdos and wore jewelry in their hair. Today we have very much the same kind of emphasis upon hair and dress. If the unsaved man you are going to marry cannot be won to Christ by your sex appeal before you marry, you will never win him to Christ by sex appeal afterward. A wife can apply a gallon of perfume and wear the thinnest negligee there is, but I tell you, she will not win him for the Lord that way.

Peter's point here is that you cannot win an unsaved man to the Lord by sex appeal.

Rather let it be the hidden person of the heart, with the incorruptible beauty of a gentle and quiet spirit, which is very precious in the sight of God. (1 Peter 3:4)

A woman is to wear an ornament, but it is to be an ornament on the inside, the ornament of a gentle and quiet spirit. In the little Book of Ruth, we read that when Boaz went into the field and saw Ruth, that beautiful maid of Moab, he fell in love with her. But have you noticed something else? Boaz had heard of her character. He had heard that she had a marvelous, wonderful character, and he fell in love with her total person.

We have many very helpful cosmetic products today, and I see nothing wrong in using anything that will make you look better. All of us want to look the best we possibly can. Alexander Pope has well advised:

> Be not the first by whom the new is tried,
> Nor yet the last to lay the old aside.[1]

Be in style. Dress up in a way that is becoming, but don't try to use that as the means of winning someone to the Lord. We need more *inward* adorning today—that is the thing that is important.

For in this manner, in former times, the holy women who trusted in God also adorned themselves, being submissive to their own husbands. (1 Peter 3:5)

There are a number of fine examples of such women in the Old Testament. I have already mentioned Ruth, who was in the genealogical line leading to Christ.

Also we are told that Rachel was a beautiful woman, and Jacob fell in love with her. She was the one bright spot in that man's life—which was a pretty dark life, by the way.

As Sarah obeyed Abraham, calling him lord, whose daughters you are if you do good and are not afraid with any terror. (1 Peter 3:6)

Sarah was such a beautiful woman that twice kings wanted her as a wife, and Abraham had a great problem in that connection. But she called Abraham *lord*. She looked up to Abraham. It is wonderful when a wife can look up to her husband.

Advice to Husbands

Now Peter speaks to husbands—

Husbands, likewise, dwell with them with understanding, giving honor to the wife, as to the weaker vessel, and as being heirs together of the grace of life, that your prayers may not be hindered. (1 Peter 3:7)

Although this seems to imply that both the husband and wife are Christians, I believe these instructions to husbands would be applicable either way.

A husband is to treat his wife as the weaker vessel, and he is to give her honor because of that. I do not think the current women's liberation movement is going to last very long. I think a woman wants to be a woman, just as a man wants to be a man. Because she is the weaker vessel, she is to be treated with honor. The man is to give first place to her. She gets into the car first as he holds the door for her. When they enter a room, she goes first. As they walk down the sidewalk, he walks on the outside for her protection. He is to treat her with honor. When a woman loses her ordained place, she does not go up; she goes down. When she takes her place, she can be treated with honor and given her rightful position. I think every husband ought to treat his wife as someone special.

"That your prayers may not be hindered." Peter says that if you are not getting along as husband and wife, it will ruin your family altar, and there is no use praying together. If you are fighting like cats and dogs—well, God just does not hear cats and dogs. But when you are in agreement, you can pray together, and your prayers will not be hindered.

CHAPTER 7

WHEN DIVORCE IS SCRIPTURAL AND MARRIAGE IS UNSCRIPTURAL

The Old Testament prophecy of Malachi reveals an age deadened to sin. The people of Israel had been drugged to an unconsciousness of sin. They were in a spiritual stupor with no conviction, which is the lowest state of sin. They mouthed surprise that God would find fault with their lifestyle. They were peevish and petulant children who affected ignorance of God's standards.

The sins of which Israel was guilty sound as familiar as the morning newspaper. You and I and our contemporary society need to hear again God's words of reproof, spoken through His man, Malachi the prophet.

Judah has dealt treacherously,
And an abomination has been committed in
  Israel and in Jerusalem,
For Judah has profaned

The LORD'S holy institution which He loves:
He has married the daughter of a foreign god.
(Malachi 2:11)

Malachi was very specific: "Judah has dealt treacherously, / and an abomination has been committed in Israel and in Jerusalem." Now we know whom Malachi was talking about: *Judah* means the tribe of Judah, *Israel* includes all the twelve tribes, and Jerusalem was the capital.

"An abomination has been committed in Israel and in Jerusalem." God was talking about how they profaned the covenant of the fathers by dealing treacherously with one another. They were profaning the holiness of the Lord. God is holy, and God loves holiness. God doesn't love sin; He hates sin.

Now God would spell it out to them. He told them specifically what He was talking about—"He [the men of Judah and Israel] has married the daughter of a foreign god." The men saw the beautiful foreign girls who lived around them when they returned from their captivity in Babylon. So they were leaving their wives and marrying these foreign girls who served pagan deities. This brought idolatry into the nation.

We see this same thing all the way through the Word of God. I believe this is the situation in Genesis 6:1–7 where we are told that the sons of God were marrying the daughters of men. I certainly do not hold the view of some expositors that the "sons of God" were angels who were cohabiting with human women and producing some sort of monstrous offspring. Our Lord expressly said that angels do not marry (see Matthew 22:30). Rather, the situation in Genesis marks the beginning of the breaking down of the godly line of Seth as they intermarried with the ungodly line of Cain.

We see this happening again when the children of Israel were nearing the promised land. The king of Moab hired Balaam to curse Israel because the king and his people, the Moabites, feared them. When God would not permit Balaam to curse them, he gave the king of Moab some very bad advice—bad for Israel. Balaam said to let the daughters of Moab marry the sons of Israel. They did intermarry, and this brought the idolatry of Moab into Israel.

Again, after the kingdom of Israel was divided, the idolatry of Phoenicia was introduced into the Northern Kingdom by the marriage of Ahab with Jezebel, the daughter of Ethbaal, who was first an idolatrous priest, then king of Tyre and Sidon.

In Malachi's Day

Now this was happening again in Malachi's day. We learn from Nehemiah that there were all kinds of pagan people living around the remnant that had returned from Babylon. A young Israelite would see some good-looking foreign girl and decide that he would like to have her for a wife. So he would get rid of his own Israelite wife and marry this pagan girl.

It is the same old story that is being reenacted in our day. I have been sounding a warning against mixed marriages (believers with unbelievers) here in southern California for more than fifty years, but the divorce rate continues to climb. Nobody is paying any attention to me, but I'll keep on saying that a believer ought not to get married to an unbeliever. Any girl or any boy who flies in the face of God's very definite and specific instructions in this connection is just flirting with trouble. Believe me, problems will be coming their way. It cannot be otherwise.

> **May the LORD cut off from the tents of Jacob**
> **The man who does this, being awake and**
>   **aware,**
> **Yet who brings an offering to the LORD of hosts!**
> (Malachi 2:12)

"The LORD cut off . . . the man who does this, being awake and aware." It doesn't make any difference who he is, he will suffer the same judgment. "Yet who brings an offering to the LORD of hosts!" Neither will he escape if he goes through the temple ritual but continues to live in sin.

My friend, a true child of God will not continue to live in sin. That is the reason the prodigal son down in the pigpen finally came to himself and said, "I will arise and go to my father." He was a son and not a pig. He had the nature of his father and could not continue to live as a pig.

I received a startling letter from a church officer here in southern California who asked for help because

he "couldn't give up the awful sin of adultery." If he
is a child of God, he will get out of the pigpen. Only
pigs love the pigpen and are satisfied to stay there.
A son will get out of it.

> **And this is the second thing you do:**
> **You cover the altar of the LORD with tears,**
> **With weeping and crying;**
> **So He does not regard the offering anymore,**
> **Nor receive it with goodwill from your hands.**
> (Malachi 2:13)

The wives of these men who were divorcing them
and marrying foreign girls came to the altar weeping. They shed their tears upon the altar, and God
said, "I heard them. Then later you came along and
very piously placed your offering upon the same altar
on which were the tears of your wives! I want you
to know that I paid no attention to your offering."

The church officer who wrote that startling letter may be the treasurer of the church or the head
deacon, but I can assure him that God is paying no
attention to his so-called good works. In fact, it
would be better for him to keep out of sight and not
go to church rather than bring reproach on the
name of Christ. God makes it very clear that He
pays no attention to his offering anymore nor receives
it with goodwill from his hands. God knows our
hypocrisy and will not accept our service.

Now the men in Malachi's day, with feigned inno-
cence and pretended ignorance, ask why:

> **Yet you say, "For what reason?"**
> **Because the LORD has been witness**

Between you and the wife of your youth,
With whom you have dealt treacherously;
Yet she is your companion
And your wife by covenant. (Malachi 2:14)

"Yet you say, 'For what reason?'" God has offended them by suggesting that He wouldn't accept their offering. The thought is that they were saying, "Why wouldn't He accept it? I brought a very nice fat lamb to offer." Malachi spells out the answer for them in neon lights so they cannot misunderstand him: "Because the LORD has been witness between you and the wife of your youth, with whom you have dealt treacherously." You see, the Israelite had married a Hebrew girl when he was a young man. But when he grew older and moved among the pagan and heathen about him, he decided that he wanted to marry one of the pagan girls whom he had learned to know.

"Yet she is your companion and your wife by covenant." His Hebrew wife was the one with whom he stood before the priest, and he covenanted to be faithful and true to her.

From the Beginning

But did He not make them one,
Having a remnant of the Spirit?
And why one?
He seeks godly offspring.
Therefore take heed to your spirit,

And let none deal treacherously with the wife of his youth. (Malachi 2:15)

"But did He not make them one?" goes back to the original creation of and institution of marriage by God Himself. Adam was a half and Eve was a half, and together they made one. This is evident when a child is born—he is part of both parents. The two are certainly one in the child.

"Having a remnant of the Spirit? And why one? He seeks godly offspring." You see, she is to be like he is—spiritually as well as physically—for the sake of the family. A home where there is divorce or where there is polygamy is not a fit place in which to raise children.

My friend, if you are a young lady, you ought not to marry that young man unless he believes as you do because, actually, you are supposed to go his way. And you will find the going rough if you are a child of God and he is not.

If you are a young person, let me say this to you. If you think that you can win your sweetheart to Christ, make sure that you do it *before* your marriage, since that is when you have the greatest influence. I tell you, a young fellow or girl in love will do almost anything to please the other. But after marriage they will not be so anxious to please. If you don't win your sweetheart to Christ before marriage, you are in trouble, and I mean *deep* trouble.

"Therefore take heed to your spirit, and let none deal treacherously with the wife of his youth." Malachi is warning them to watch what they are doing. God had specifically forbidden His people to intermarry with the unbelievers.

> **"For the LORD God of Israel says**
> **That He hates divorce,**
> **For it covers one's garment with violence,"**
> **Says the LORD of hosts.**
> **"Therefore take heed to your spirit,**
> **That you do not deal treacherously."**
> (Malachi 2:16)

In the Old Testament, when a man married a girl he took his outer garment and put it over her. This lovely custom was to signify that he was going to protect her.

This is what Boaz did for Ruth. Ruth was a widow and, according to the Mosaic Law, she had to claim Boaz as her kinsman redeemer before he could act. He could not ask her to marry him; she had to claim him. So her mother-in-law, Naomi, acting like a regular matchmaker, sent Ruth down to the threshing floor. It was harvesttime, and all the families were camped around the threshing floor. At night, to protect the grain, the men slept around it with their heads toward the heap of grain and their feet stuck out like spokes of a wheel. Ruth followed Naomi's instructions and lay at the feet of Boaz. During the night he realized that someone was there and asked who it was. She replied, "I am Ruth, your maidservant. Spread the corner of your garment over your maidservant [in other words, take your maidservant under your wing] for you are a close relative." She was asking him to marry her. In marriage a man offers a woman his protection and his love and she offers her devotion and her life to him. This is a beautiful picture of Christ's relationship with believers.

In Malachi's day the men of Israel were dealing treacherously with their wives. They had covered them with their garments in marriage, but now they were covering their garment with violence. In other words, they had divorced their wives.

Notice that God says He *hates* divorce—"He hates divorce, for it covers one's garment with violence."

God's Ideal

God's ideal for man from the very beginning was that there should be no divorce. We know that, for Jesus said that Moses allowed divorce because of the hardness of men's hearts, but that from the beginning it was not so. Then how was it at the beginning?

So Adam gave names to all cattle, to the birds of the air, and to every beast of the field. But for Adam there was not found a helper comparable to him. (Genesis 2:20)

To begin with, we learn that among all the creation of God that was beneath man, none could take the place of what God would create for Adam—that is, a wife. God had created all other creatures by twos. God let Adam give names to all the animals so that he would discover for himself that each animal had a mate but that he was alone and needed someone who was like he was but yet different from him. He needed one who was a helper, someone to be fitted to him. He was just a half, and he needed the other half there so that together they could be one. That was the thing God had in mind. God created Adam first and allowed him time to realize that he needed someone else.

And the LORD God caused a deep sleep to fall on Adam, and he slept; and He took one of his ribs, and closed up the flesh in its place. (Genesis 2:21)

Why did God do that? Why didn't He take her from the ground as He had done with Adam? Because she was to be like Adam and yet different from him. She must come from man because man is not really a whole person. She was made from his side. This is not some foolish story. God wants to impress upon man that woman is part of man, that he is only half a man without a woman.

The Scriptures know nothing about this idea of either women's lib or the other extreme, the inferiority of women. God put woman on a high plane. It is obvious to us already that the people in the days of Malachi had lost that vision. That is why God was admonishing them, "When you sin against the wife of your youth, you are sinning against Me." God protects the status of women.

And Adam said:
"This is now bone of my bones
And flesh of my flesh;

**She shall be called Woman,
Because she was taken out of Man."**
(Genesis 2:23)

What is woman? Adam was *ish*, and woman is *isha*. She is the other side or other half of the male. We call them male and female. She is "bone of my bones and flesh of my flesh." She is called woman because she was taken out of man.

And they were both naked, the man and his wife, and were not ashamed. (Genesis 2:25)

This was before sin had entered into the world. Neither one looked with lust upon the other because at that time they were innocent. They looked upon each other with tenderness and with love. There was a mutual respect. Each of them could truly say, "You are the one for me." The creation of Eve made Adam a man, all man. The presence of Adam made Eve a woman, all woman.

I really get provoked when I hear people talk as if sex is something that is bad. Of course, the sex act outside of marriage is wrong. But after all, who was it that thought of sex? God is the One who thought of it and made it. He is the One who designed man and woman. He had in mind a marvelous arrangement when He created the sexes.

Why Divorce Was Permitted

Then sin entered into the world, and it marred everything, including the relationship in marriage.

When we get to the time of Moses and the Law, we find that divorce was permitted. This does not mean that it was God's intention when He instituted marriage, but He permitted it, as Jesus said, because of the hardness of man's heart. The Mosaic Law said this:

> **When a man takes a wife and marries her, and it happens that she finds no favor in his eyes because he has found some uncleanness in her, and he writes her a certificate of divorce, puts it in her hand, and sends her out of his house. . . .** (Deuteronomy 24:1)

"Uncleanness" in the bride may imply that she had deceived her husband by not being what she claimed to be. When, for instance, her husband found that she was not a virgin, then he could write her a bill of divorcement.

By the time of the New Testament, the interpretation of *uncleanness* had become so broad that if a wife even burned the biscuits, that would be grounds for divorce. At the time that Jesus was asked the question, "Is it lawful for a man to divorce his wife for just any reason?" the rabbis were teaching that a wife could be divorced upon the slightest whim, which was certainly contrary to the intent of the Mosaic Law.

There were other specifics in this Mosaic Law:

> **When she has departed from his house, and goes and becomes another man's wife, if the latter husband detests her and writes her a**

certificate of divorce, puts it in her hand, and sends her out of his house, or if the latter husband dies who took her as his wife, then her former husband who divorced her must not take her back to be his wife after she has been defiled; for that is an abomination before the LORD, and you shall not bring sin on the land which the LORD your God is giving you as an inheritance. (Deuteronomy 24:2–4)

That would be progressive prostitution, and it would lead to the sort of thing we are seeing in our contemporary society, people being married and divorced seven or eight times! To do that is absolutely to ridicule the marriage vow.

Jesus on Divorce

The problem that was prevalent in Israel at the time of Malachi is prevalent in our contemporary culture today. We have certainly changed our viewpoint on divorce in recent years in this country. I suppose that divorce is one of the most controversial subjects that any Bible teacher has to deal with today because there is confusion as to what the Bible really says on that problem, and there is a great difference and wide diversity of interpretation. You cannot say that there are *no* grounds for divorce, although that was the unanimous decision of the church over a century ago—in spite of what the Word of God had to say.

The Lord Jesus made two things very clear on this subject of divorce.

1. Moses had permitted divorce because of the hardness of heart of the people.
2. There is one clear-cut basis for divorce, and that is fornication, unfaithfulness to the marriage vow on the part of either the man or the woman.

Notice this record in Matthew's Gospel:

The Pharisees also came to Him, testing Him, and saying to Him, "Is it lawful for a man to divorce his wife for just any reason?" And He answered and said to them, "Have you not read that He who made them at the beginning 'made them male and female,' and said, 'For this reason a man shall leave his father and mother and be joined to his wife, and the two shall become one flesh'?" (Matthew 19:3–5)

As I mentioned before, Jesus goes back to the beginning, to the time of creation, when God instituted marriage.

"So then, they are no longer two but one flesh. Therefore what God has joined together, let not man separate." They said to Him, "Why then did Moses command to give a certificate of divorce, and to put her away?" He said to them, "Moses, because of the hardness of your

hearts, permitted you to divorce your wives, but from the beginning it was not so." (Matthew 19:6–8)

Then He sets down the one reason for which divorce is allowed:

"And I say to you, whoever divorces his wife, except for sexual immorality, and marries another, commits adultery; and whoever marries her who is divorced commits adultery." (Matthew 19:9)

It is quite interesting how the disciples followed up that statement with this conclusion:

His disciples said to Him, "If such is the case of the man with his wife, it is better not to marry." (Matthew 19:10)

In other words, "If it is really that strict, if there is one and only one reason for divorce, then it would be better not to get married at all."

Then our Lord explained the liberty that we have:

But He said to them, "All cannot accept this saying, but only those to whom it has been given: For there are eunuchs who were born thus from their mother's womb, and there are eunuchs who were made eunuchs by men, and there are eunuchs who have made themselves eunuchs for the kingdom of heaven's sake. He who is able to accept it, let him accept it." (Matthew 19:11–12)

It is not necessary for everyone to get married. There are some men and some women who do not need to marry. By no means is it a sin to be single. Some folk simply do not need to get married—they are eunuchs from birth. Others are made eunuchs by man, such as Daniel in the court of Nebuchadnezzar. It was forced upon them and served the purpose of making captives more docile toward the king, and it also enabled them to devote more time to their studies. Then there are eunuchs for the kingdom of heaven's sake. That is, there are individuals who have kept themselves eunuchs in order to serve the cause of Christ and the cause of the church. It is wonderful if a man or a woman feels able to do that. I have known several preachers who have never married. I thought I would do the same in my ministry and decided that I would be an old bachelor all my life. But I soon learned that bachelorhood wasn't for me. This is an area in which God has given us great liberty. But the important thing is this: Christ said that if you do choose to get married, it is a commitment. The only ground for divorce is fornication by your mate.

Paul on Marriage

In the days of the early church this matter of fornication arose in the Corinthian church. People of different religious backgrounds were in the church, and there were couples who had married when they were pagans, but later one of the spouses became a Christian. What should have been their relationship after one of them was converted? Paul addressed this new situation:

Now to the married I command, yet not I but the Lord: A wife is not to depart from her husband. But even if she does depart, let her remain unmarried or be reconciled to her husband. And a husband is not to divorce his wife. (1 Corinthians 7:10–11)

If a couple had been married when they were pagans and now one is converted to Christianity, the Christian is not to walk out on the marriage. If the believer departs, he is to remain unmarried or else be reconciled again.

But to the rest I, not the Lord, say: If any brother has a wife who does not believe, and she is willing to live with him, let him not divorce her. And a woman who has a husband who does not believe, if he is willing to live with her, let her not divorce him. For the unbelieving husband is sanctified by the wife, and the unbelieving wife is sanctified by the husband; otherwise your children would be unclean, but now they are holy. But if the unbeliever departs, let him depart; a brother or a sister is not under bondage in such cases. But God has called us to peace. (1 Corinthians 7:12–15)

Although Jesus said that fornication is the only cause for divorce, the pagan member of a marriage may want to walk out on the marriage. After the partner becomes a believer, the unsaved party may say, "I don't like this arrangement. Things are different now from when I married you. I'm going to leave." In such a case Paul says to let the unbeliever go. Whether the unbeliever goes out and gets married again or not, in this situation I assume it would mean that the believing husband or wife would be free to marry again.

When Paul said, "A brother or a sister is not under bondage in such cases," what is the bondage? It is the marriage vows.

When he said, "God has called us to peace," I believe Paul was saying that God does not ask any man or woman to live in a *hell* at home. Never. If they find that they cannot get along together, that they fight like cats and dogs, I think they ought to separate. On several occasions I have advised couples to separate—but neither of them is to remarry. Their problem is not divorce, it is marriage. They should not have married in the first place. God has called us to peace, therefore the home is not to be a boxing ring nor a place for karate. It is a place for *love*.

There Is Forgiveness

A home of love is God's ideal for man. From the beginning God did not intend for divorce to be part of the equation, but because of man's sin, He permitted it. You may say, "Well, divorce is sinful."

Sure it is, and so is murder. But a murderer can be saved. In fact, one was dying on a cross next to Jesus, and he was saved. When Jesus Christ died on the cross, He died for all sins. The thief on the cross was both a thief and a murderer, and his faith in the Lord Jesus Christ and His shed blood saved him. A thief can be saved, and a divorced person can be saved, too. So let's not put divorce in a special category all by itself. If an unsaved person has been a thief and then repents and gets saved by coming to Jesus Christ, he is forgiven for his thievery. We would permit such a man to get married. We would do the same for a murderer. Then let us be fair about divorce. There are people who get divorced before they are saved. When they come to the Lord Jesus Christ, they are forgiven for that sin. I think such a person is free to marry again, and I feel that this is implied in the Scriptures.

CHAPTER 8

WHAT JESUS SAID ABOUT DIVORCE

For many years now the divorce rate has been increasing at an alarming pace. A statistician wryly remarked, "Before long we're going to have more divorces than we have marriages if the present trend continues." I do not want to be tedious by quoting a long list of statistics, but they certainly present a very bleak picture concerning the subject of marriage and divorce.

Every informed person is aware that there is a storm blowing just now over the sea of matrimony. Rough seas greet every couple who set out upon the voyage of life. The shore is lined with broken ships wrecked in this dangerous age of low morals and easy living. Each one of the couples will tell you they sailed out on a fair day. The sky was clear, the sea was calm, but they soon encountered the rolling waves. The opposing wind began to blow upon them, and they found themselves without chart or compass to guide them.

There is not at this present time a family who has not been affected in some way by divorce. There is not a person reading this who doesn't have a relative, perhaps several relatives, who have been involved in divorce. That's true of me, and I'm sure it is true of you.

Actually, our problem today is not centered on the question of divorce at all. I think that has been one of our big mistakes. The question really centers on the subject of marriage. The spotlight has been put on the divorce court when it should be put on the marriage altar. We decry the evil of divorce today, and yet we approve every wedding.

Warn Them

You would never, my friend, send an ocean liner out to sea manned by a group of Cub Scouts. Nor would you want to fly across the Atlantic with a crew made up of Girl Scouts. Yet today there are couples who are starting out on the voyage of matrimony equally ill equipped for it.

A church that has adopted harsh rules on divorce and pays no attention to the training of young people for marriage is at best being highly inconsistent. Why do we preachers stand in the pulpit and talk against divorce and then marry every couple that knocks at our door? Even our highway department puts up a warning before you get to the sharp curve in the road. And a red flag *should* be put up at the time the wedding is first announced rather than waiting until the wreck takes place around the curve. But we act as though it's all right to condemn divorce *per se*, although we've given no instruction for marriage at all.

It's not at the divorce trial that we're having our trouble today, it's the fact that there are folk getting married without being alerted to the perils ahead. Someone says, "It's too bad so-and-so is getting a divorce." My friend, it's too bad they got married! That's where the mistake was made—and is being made with multitudes of folk. Let me change the metaphor a little: We are locking the stable after the horse is gone.

When I first became pastor at a downtown church, a couple came to me and asked that I perform their marriage ceremony. As I talked with them I became confident that they would not have a successful marriage. They were amazed and actually became angry when I refused to perform the ceremony. In fact, the parents of the girl were so angry with me that for several years they would not even speak to me.

May I say to you that in less than two years that girl asked for an interview. She was altogether a different person when she asked to see me. She had *had* it. She was a humbled girl, and she said, "I made a mistake. What shall I do?" "Well," I said, "I wish you had asked that question two years ago when I told you that from my viewpoint as a preacher and from Scripture you should not get married— that you could not make a go of it. You said you could. You have gone ahead and proven that you could not make it work, and now you want to know what to do. Well, it's too late now to salvage anything. The ship is already wrecked." And it *was* already wrecked. We need to give a warning today, and the warning should not be about divorce but about marriage.

A man and his wife were sitting on the porch swing late one summer evening back in the Middle West. It was a hot night and they were waiting for it to cool off enough to go to bed. As they sat there in the darkness, their daughter drove up with her "steady," and they got out of the car. He ushered her up to the porch and, lo and behold, the fellow chose that time to propose to the girl, not realizing that her parents were there on the porch. The parents were greatly embarrassed, of course, and the wife reached over and whispered to her husband, "Do you think we ought to warn them?" And he said, "Oh, no, nobody warned me!" Well, friend, today we do need to warn them.

Reasons for Divorce

Now our Lord placed the emphasis upon marriage and not upon divorce. And the question is, what did He really say about this question? The first occasion on which our Lord spoke about this subject was in what is commonly called the Sermon on the Mount:

Furthermore it has been said, "Whoever divorces his wife, let him give her a certificate

of divorce." But I say to you that whoever divorces his wife for any reason except sexual immorality causes her to commit adultery; and whoever marries a woman who is divorced commits adultery. (Matthew 5:31–32)

I'm not going to deal with that at all now because from my interpretation of Scripture, the Sermon on the Mount finds its final fruition in the day that's yet ahead, the Millennium. Now don't be distressed when I say that, for our Lord, in chapter 19 of Matthew, says the identical thing concerning marriage and divorce. This particular chapter has an extended and full statement of our Lord on this subject.

The Pharisees also came to Him, testing Him, and saying to Him, "Is it lawful for a man to divorce his wife for just any reason?" (Matthew 19:3)

Notice that the Lord Jesus did not introduce the subject. His enemies—at this time, the Pharisees—introduced it, and they did not introduce it in a friendly manner. The question was not asked for the purpose of inquiry or actually of getting an answer. It was for the same reason that a great many folk today will try to put the preacher on the spot. They like to do that by asking a question that is divisive, and I realize we are dealing with what is very debatable in our day also. That was as live an issue in Christ's day as it is in our day. I have a feeling that this question of marriage and divorce has been around from the day that Adam sinned in the Garden of Eden down to the present hour, and it will continue to be even through the Millennium.

Notice what these men did. They came with this question that a newspaper reporter today would call a hot subject. At that particular time, Herod Antipas had divorced his wife and had married the wife of his brother Philip. It was an open scandal. John the Baptist was beheaded because of his comments on that subject. That's what could happen to a preacher when he talks on a subject like this! The case of Herod Antipas marrying the wife of his brother Philip was an awful, sordid thing, and there was a great deal of discussion on it.

Now the deceitful Pharisees were baiting the trap for our Lord Jesus. They were hopelessly divided among themselves on this subject. There was confusion, and the confusion centered around the Mosaic Law. Moses had written:

> **When a man takes a wife and marries her, and it happens that she finds no favor in his eyes because he has found some uncleanness in her, and he writes her a certificate of divorce, puts it in her hand, and sends her out of his house. . . .** (Deuteronomy 24:1)

If you will check the Gospel of Mark on this, you'll find that the woman was given the same option:

> **And if a woman divorces her husband and marries another, she commits adultery.** (Mark 10:12)

You see, the Law has a way of referring to the party of the first part as "he," when sometimes the party of the first part is a she. The Mosaic Law did that, but generally the term is generic when the Greek *anthropos* is used. It means *mankind*, and may apply to either man or woman.

Now here was a case, if you please, where the Law of Moses said that a man could divorce his wife, and apparently he could divorce her for causes other than that of adultery. As a result, there were two schools of interpretation and the question was: What did Moses really mean?

First was the school of Hillel, and Hillel's school was the most prominent. He had died about twenty years before our Lord was born. He was a great teacher, who upheld that which would correspond today to incompatibility as a reason for divorce. Then he added a whole list of specific rules, and they're rather amusing. One of them was that if the wife left salt out of the bread it would be a just cause for divorce. In fact, some of the grounds that were allowed were ridiculous, but after all, aren't some of the grounds ridiculous that are used for divorce in our society?

Then there was the other school, the school of Shammi. He said there was only one reason for divorce, and that was adultery. May I say, I think he was wrong in his interpretation of Moses because the penalty for adultery was handled by Moses in a different manner. In the case of adultery the guilty party was stoned to death—always. There were no ifs, ands, or buts about it in that day. The guilty party was stoned to death. So evidently what Moses meant in Deuteronomy 24:1 was that there were other justifiable causes for divorce. Therefore, both Hillel and Shammi were presenting the extreme views, and neither one dealt with what Moses had in mind.

Now, what did Moses mean? The Pharisees came to the Lord Jesus and said to Him, "Is it lawful for a man to divorce his wife for just any reason?" It's obvious what they had in mind. They were thinking of Herod's case and comparing what Moses said with Shammi's interpretation and Hillel's interpretation. Which one is right? Which one are we to follow?

This is without a doubt one of the most amazing procedures that our Lord ever followed when He was here. Christ ignored both Hillel and Shammi. He didn't pay a bit of attention to them at all. Listen to Him:

> **And He answered and said to them, "Have you not read that He who made them at the beginning 'made them male and female,' and said, 'For this reason a man shall leave his father and mother and be joined to his wife, and the two shall become one flesh'?"** (Matthew 19:4–5)

And the most shocking thing of all is that our Lord also passed by Moses! He ignored Moses. When they came to Him and said, "Is it lawful to divorce your wife for just any reason?" our Lord ignored Hillel and Shammi—somehow or other we can explain that— but why did He ignore the writings of Moses?

Do you see what He was doing? He took the emphasis off divorce and put it back on marriage. He went back to the origin of marriage, back to the very beginning, back to God's ideal for mankind. He went back to the Garden of Eden before sin entered that garden. He went back to when God created man and what God had in mind when He created him. God created them male and female. He didn't create two men and one woman. He didn't create two women and one man. It sure would have been bad for Adam if he hadn't liked Eve, wouldn't it? There was one man and one woman. Our Lord went back to that ideal.

Divorce and the Children

It is interesting that our Lord, having spoken about the issue of divorce, immediately begins to talk about children. The children are all-important in any divorce. In the parallel passage to Matthew 19 over in Mark 10:13–16, it says:

Then they brought little children to Him, that He might touch them; but the disciples rebuked those who brought them. But when Jesus saw it, He was greatly displeased and said to them, "Let the little children come to Me, and do not forbid them; for of such is the kingdom of God. Assuredly, I say to you, whoever does not receive the kingdom of God as a little

**child will by no means enter it." And He took
them up in His arms, laid His hands on them,
and blessed them.**

A woman once came to me wanting a divorce
because she no longer loved her husband. She said,
"Because of all the things he is doing, I no longer
love him, and I have heard you say that when there
is no love, there is no relationship. So I want to get
a divorce."

It is true that when there is no love, there is no
relationship, and that is very sad, but that is not
the basis for divorce. I said to this woman, "You
tell me that you don't love your husband, but do
you love your children?" She said, "Of course I do,
but what has that got to do with it?" I told her that
it has everything to do with it. "You are to stay
with him as long as you can if you love those children."

My friend, the fact that our Lord said, "Let the
little children come to Me," ought to tell any couple, especially a Christian couple, to make every
effort to hold their marriage together. A great per-
centage of children and young folk who are in
trouble with the law come from broken homes.
And you would be surprised to learn the number
of little ones who have been turned away from
Christ because of their divorced parents. How
tragic! It is very significant that Jesus ties together
the subject of divorce and His loving concern for
children.

What About Mama?

May I say to you, my beloved, that our Lord revealed the solemn sanctity and high level of marriage. He went so far as to say that the oneness relationship that exists between a parent and a child is broken by marriage. Oh, that's tremendous. Today the loveliest pictures are the ones of a mother holding a little baby. What a sweet relationship! Father and son—what a picture! But there comes a day when that boy and that girl get married, and when they do, the singular relationship to the parent is broken. And for goodness sake, Mama, stay home and let them alone. You may think liquor is the cause today of more divorces than anything else, but I tell you, Mama is the cause of a great many.

Let me give you another case. Some time back a mother-in-law came to me and told me about her son-in-law who was beating her daughter, so that she was actually black and blue. It was awful. The girl's mother said, "I've come all the way out from Illinois in order to do something about this." So I said, "Will the couple talk to me together?" She said, "I think they will. I have really talked to them."

And they did come. The mother-in-law had told me that he was an unsaved fellow—and he was, but a nice fellow. I said to him, "Have you beaten her?" And he said, "Yeah. I'm ashamed of myself, but I did." I said, "Why did you do it?" "Well," he said, "look, her mother came out, and we live in a trailer and we just didn't have room for her, but she came anyway. And she and my wife here ganged up on me." I asked the girl, "Is that right?" She said, "Yes, we did." And he said, "I'm not a very good talker, but both of them are and, honestly, I had no comeback. I shouldn't have done it, but that's all I could do. I had to hit somebody."

I said to him, "Look, fellow, I have to begin at the beginning—there's no use my trying to straighten you out yet. You know you need Jesus Christ as your Savior. Would you accept Him?" Well, he had no argument at all. He said he would receive Christ, and he did. We got down on our knees and prayed. I said, "That's wonderful. I think you will make a go of it now. Don't you think you can?" She was weeping, and he was weeping and they said they could.

Then I asked the mother-in-law to come back to see me. When she came in she said, "I want to thank you, Dr. McGee, for what you did," and all of that sort of thing.

I said, "Well, I don't know whether you're going to appreciate what I'm about to say to you."

She interrupted, "What are you going to say?"

"Did you buy a return ticket to Chicago?"

"Yes, I did."

"If I were you, I'd use it in the next twenty-four hours."

"How dare you tell me!"

"Wait a minute, you had me tell your daughter and son-in-law, now I'm telling you. Go home!" She doesn't like me to this day, but she went home.

That couple has made a go of it, and they will continue making a go of it. You see, the mother was the trouble. Our Lord says the relationship between you and your father and mother is broken at the time of your marriage. Isn't that wonderful! That makes marriage one of the most sacred relationships there is.

Father's Permission

Now our Lord says, and will you listen to Him carefully,

So then, they are no longer two but one flesh. Therefore what God has joined together, let not man separate. (Matthew 19:6)

Our Lord comes down from the lofty mountaintop to sea level where marriages live—the sea of matrimony. If a man or woman leaves father and mother for the lofty plane and sanctity of the marital relationship, if that ideal is attained, let not anyone "put that asunder."

What He's saying is that it's all right to go and ask the father's permission to marry the girl, but he may be the wrong father. First ask your heavenly Father. He's the One you are to get permission from. My friend, marriages are made in heaven or hell—there is no third place. When marriage is made in the wrong place, it is in trouble to begin with. Even Christians find that marriage becomes a very shaky proposition.

Why Was Divorce Permitted?

Now we come to the real objection. The Pharisees are on their toes.

> **They said to Him, "Why then did Moses command to give a certificate of divorce, and to put her away?"** (Matthew 19:7)

If marriage is on such a high plane, then why did Moses permit divorce? Will you listen to our Lord?

> **He said to them, "Moses, because of the hardness of your hearts, permitted you to divorce your wives, but from the beginning it was not so."** (Matthew 19:8)

He said the reason that divorce was ever permitted was because of the hardness of your heart. Now wait just a minute, hardness toward one another? Oh, no. Hardness toward God. When man sinned in the Garden of Eden and lost his relationship with God, he became hard toward God. Listen to Adam talk back to God. Look at Cain as he insulted God. Follow the record of man to the Flood and the Tower of Babel. Follow him on and look at him today in your town. Man is hard toward God. And, my friend, when you are hard toward God, you cannot have the tenderness that God can give you toward your spouse. No, you can't. You can show sexual love, but you cannot reach the high and holy plane that God has for you until you are tender with God and rightly related to Him. When men were not rightly related with God, then Moses permitted divorce.

The Lord Jesus said,

And I say to you, whoever divorces his wife, except for sexual immorality, and marries another, commits adultery; and whoever marries her who is divorced commits adultery. (Matthew 19:9)

The one ground for divorce is unfaithfulness to the marriage vow. Our Lord said that back at the beginning there was God's ideal. That ideal was broken, broken by man's sin, and since man is in sin he doesn't always attain the ideal. So many couples enter marriage without that in mind. They don't seek God's strength to help them bring it up to that level. As a result God's ideal is not attained, and when God's ideal is not attained, divorce usually follows. What else could come out of it because of the hardness of your heart?

May I say to you, my beloved, be careful about condemning those who were divorced before they were saved. Some of us are so wrong here and so unkind and unlovely in pointing our finger at some unfortunate person who got a divorce and even married again before being saved. When did you get better than God? Don't you know that God forgave them when they came to Christ? That hardness of the heart toward God has now been taken away, and they are now new creations in Christ. Are you going to point your finger at them and say that they're out of the will of God?

A confused, distracted woman come to see me for counseling, and this was her story: As a girl back in the Middle West in a godless home, she had run away with a fellow. He later deserted her when their first baby was born. Then she met another man, a professional man. They married and moved to California where they both were saved. I've been in their home. It's a lovely home, and they have fine children. But a preacher had the audacity to tell her that she ought to leave that husband and go back to the man in the Middle West who was an alcoholic. May I say to you, that kind of talk and that kind of thinking have absolutely missed what our Lord had in mind. That's another example of hardness of the heart. I'm just wondering if some of us don't have hardness of heart toward others, especially toward folk like this. It's so easy to point the finger.

I have pastored a church that had the rule that if you've been divorced you cannot serve the Lord in the church. How ridiculous! If a man has been a murderer and gets saved, we would let him come to the platform and give a testimony. But if in the past before he was saved he had had a divorce, he wouldn't be permitted to give a testimony. I personally know some of these folk who have remarried and have established homes that are much more Christlike than many who have never been involved in a divorce. Oh, my friend, our Lord says it's because of the hardness of our hearts that this ungraciousness has come about. But when a divorced person comes to Christ, it's a different story and a new beginning.

What Is Unfaithfulness?

Now let me move on from here. Our Lord says that because of the sacredness of marriage there is only one ground for divorce, which is unfaithfulness. However, I want to tell you that unfaithfulness has many angles. For a while I averaged about one hundred couples a year who came to me for counseling. And, oh, the different stories they told! Unfaithfulness can manifest itself in many ways. Many a wife is not doing her part in the marriage, and many a husband is not doing his part in the marriage, and when they don't carry out their parts, they are being unfaithful. My friend, unfaithfulness takes many turns.

May I give just one example of what I'm trying to say. I talked with a couple—he was unsaved, she was saved—and under very careful questioning she admitted that she had kept herself from him, physically, on purpose. She knew as an unsaved man and given his nature he would break the marriage vow with adultery. And he did. So she got a divorce on those grounds. I say to you, she was wrong. Technically, no. But that's what I mean by saying there can be a lot of things involved. I said to her, "You have no scriptural grounds to stand on at all in this matter."

The High Plane of Marriage

Now, let's pick up again in Matthew 19. His disciples said to Him, "If such is the case of the man with his wife, it is better not to marry" (Matthew 19:10).

I wish more young people had this high and holy notion of marriage. Instead, they become too intimate, let their emotions run away, and get married before they're ready for it. Then they wonder what happened. Oh, my friend, because marriage is so tremendously sacred and on such a high plane, you had better be dead sure you are able to reach that plane when you get married. The trouble is not only that people are getting divorced today, but the greater problem is that there are young and not-so-young people getting married who ought not to get married. Now don't misunderstand me. I am certainly not advocating sex without marriage. That is an entirely different subject.

This is how our Lord responded to the disciples' statement:

> **But He said to them, "All cannot accept this saying, but only those to whom it has been given: For there are eunuchs who were born thus from their mother's womb, and there are eunuchs who were made eunuchs by men, and there are eunuchs who have made themselves eunuchs for the kingdom of heaven's sake. He who is able to accept it, let him accept it."** (Matthew 19:11–12)

Our Lord is saying that although you can't make it a rule, there is a great principle involved here. He said let the one who can receive it, receive it if it's for him.

For example, if you are in God's work, you may be called to go to a certain mission field, and marriage could be an issue. One of our missionaries discussed this with me when she finished school. She said, "Dr. McGee, my chances of getting married when I go to the mission field are nil. What shall I do?" And I said to her, "If you're able to do it, you go ahead and go to the mission field. If you're not, if singleness is not for you, don't go." She came back later and said, "It is for me." And that's a sacrifice she has made. There are a lot of folk who have made that decision. But it's not for everybody.

One church has made a rule that its priests be celibate, but the Lord said, "He who is able to accept it, let him accept it." And if you can receive it, receive it. Remember that the Bible tells us, "Marriage is honorable among all" (Hebrews 13:4), so we can't make celibacy a rule. Oh, how we like to make a few little rules—it's like making a hoop and asking everybody to jump through our little hoop. Marriage is so high and holy that you need to examine your own heart to make sure you can enter into it on God's plane.

Marriage is the most sacred relationship in this life. The only relationship greater than marriage is the relationship of your soul to Jesus Christ.

A young wisecracker came to me with this: "You know, Dr. McGee, love is blind, marriage is an institution, so marriage is an institution for the blind." Young person, you had better not be blind when you enter it, because God has put marriage on such a high and holy plane.

Paul likened the marriage relationship to Christ and His church. He says, "Husbands, love your wives, just as Christ also loved the church and gave Himself for her" (Ephesians 5:25). He said, "Wives, submit to your own husbands, as to the Lord" (Ephesians 5:22). Until marriage reaches that relationship, it's not His ideal. There are many today who are just getting by. They don't represent God in their marriages at all.

I'm not so concerned about those who have already gotten married—it's too late to warn them. And I'm not so much concerned about those who have been divorced, to tell the truth. If they had just grounds for it or they divorced before they were saved, you and I have no right to point a finger of condemnation at them. But I tell you frankly, I am concerned about those contemplating marriage in these days. If this includes you, *you* are the one who concerns me.

Are you prepared for it? Are you ready to get married?

"Oh, but we've fallen in love, and he's such a great guy."

Are you ready to bring it up to God's high level?

"Oh, but she's so pretty."

Are you able to come up to God's exalted plane? A man shall leave his father and mother and cleave to his wife. Back in the beginning, God made them for one another. You'd better be sure that your choice is your heavenly Father's choice for you. Marriage is sacred. Don't enter it until you are ready to enter.

Our Lord said, "Let him that can receive it, receive it." But marriage is honorable, and if you can bring it up to this level then you go ahead and get married.

The Savior's Love

Marriage is difficult under any circumstances, but in this day it's tremendously difficult. As you look about you, the marriages you see may not mirror what they should. They ought to mirror the relationship of Christ and the church. But if the ones you've seen do not mirror that, then look above them to a Savior who has a *real* love for you. Remember the first time you saw your beloved and fell in love? Wasn't it wonderful? Well, there's a Savior today who loves you, and you are *not* wonderful to Him. No, you're not. You are a sinner, and yet He loves you unconditionally, loves you more than you could ever love anyone, and He wants to save you— and He can. He will bring you into the body of believers so that someday He can present you to His Father without spot or blemish, His holy bride! What a relationship—a relationship of genuine love. That's what heaven is going to be, a place for Christ and His bride.

CHAPTER 9

THE GREATEST LOVE SONG IN ALL THE WORLD

The Song of Solomon could be called, I suppose, a lyric poem. Solomon was the Stephen Foster, the Irving Berlin, and the Andrew Lloyd-Weber of his day. We're told back in 1 Kings 4:32, "He spoke three thousand proverbs"—we have only a few hundred of them—"and his songs were one thousand and five." We have only one of the thousand and five songs that he wrote. But do not be distressed by this loss, for the very simple reason that we have the best one. It is called the Song of Songs, and that's the Hebrew way of saying, "This is the best one he wrote."

Now, the Song of Solomon has always been a disturbing factor in the thinking of believers down through the years because it was written in the elaborate, vivid, and passionate language of the ancient East. It's painted with bold strokes in bright colors, and there are no neutral tints in this book. It's actually delightful, delirious, and a divine perfume when we enter into it, but our occidental minds are offended by its uncensored expressions. And there is a danger, of course, of reading into it the vulgar and voluptuous, the sexual and the sensuous.

Also, the Song of Solomon has been used by the critics to find fault with the Word of God. But Origen and Jerome tell us that the young Israelite was not permitted to read the Song of Solomon until he was thirty years of age. And that, by the way, was a very good procedure.

There have always been diverse viewpoints as to the interpretation of this book. I think it's very important to see that the German critical viewpoint, which so many hold today, is not satisfactory at all. The view I'm following is by no means original with me, but it is the interpretation that satisfies my own heart.

Although I have preached on the Song of Solomon many times, I must confess to you that it means a great deal more to me today than it did twenty years ago. If you will compare this poem to other poems and songs that came out of the Orient during the same period, you will find that this one is extremely mild and restrained. Actually it's not as elaborate as the others, nor is it as vivid as it appears to our occidental minds.

The Glory of Love

When you approach the Song of Solomon, you are coming to the holy of holies. As was true of the

Holy of Holies in the temple, that not everyone was permitted inside its sacred enclosure, so it is with the Song of Solomon—you are dwelling in the secret place of the Most High. And the skeptic, the carnal Christian, the man of the world is apt to say, "Well, what good purpose does this book serve? Does it have any practical value?" The pragmatist says today when he comes to this, "Can you articulate a book like this into life?"

Married Love

May I say to you that this book just happens to be a little more practical than the pragmatist thinks it is. It sets forth, first of all, the glory of wedded love. Also, my friend, it has a message for you and me regarding one of the most important phases of our lives, which is the sacredness of marriage. It teaches us that marriage is a divine institution in spite of what the media are doing to it in our day. The Song of Songs teaches what real love is. It reveals the heart of a satisfied husband and devoted wife. As you know, this generation in which we live boasts of its sophistication and knows a great deal about sex, but it knows practically nothing about real love. Witness the divorces of today. These shallow folk in the entertainment world who are so attractive to the eye can't live together very long. Why? They know all about sex, but they know nothing about real love. Solomon's Song is a book that ought to be a primer today for young couples who are entering into the state of matrimony.

The old anecdote is told about the father who took his son aside and said, "Son, I want to talk to you about the birds and the bees." And the son responded, "Sure, Dad, what is it you want to know?" Unfortunately we are living in a day when a boy or girl of thirteen knows more than the parents know about sexual matters.

A veteran movie queen today may have had five husbands, but she's ignorant of real love. In our modern novels and plays, the heroes are neurotic, the heroines are erotic, and the plots are tommyrotic. Our media are taking folk through the moral sewers of life. And who would like to make a trip tomorrow through the sewers of Los Angeles or New York? It's not a very enticing or engaging trip, my beloved. And so in stark contrast this Song of Solomon sets before us the beauty and the glory of marriage.

Jehovah's Love for Israel

The second thing this little book does is to set before us the love of Jehovah for Israel. And this is where the Old Testament saints, especially the rabbis, found so much rich meaning. That theme was not new to them—the prophets had presented this in many, many Scripture portions. Hosea especially speaks of the fact that Jehovah is the bridegroom and the nation Israel is the bride.

Christ's Love for the Church

Also, the church today has found rich meaning in this little book. It reveals the love of Christ for the church. God, knowing your difficulty and my difficulty, uses human affection, that which we personally understand, to convey spiritual truth to our dull minds, our discontented hearts, our distorted affections, and our diseased wills. In this beautiful love song He portrays something of His great love for us. This is the way He does it, and this is how practical it is.

God's so great love is brought down to a human plane where you and I can grasp it and then be elevated and lifted to the very heights. God uses a little book like this to arouse us—arouse you and arouse me—to respond to His love and to love Him in return.

Christ's Love for Me!

Then may I say there's a fourth and last wonderful meaning in this book. Many have made it very personal. They have found in this book the love of Christ for themselves, for the individual. Some of the greatest saints the church has ever produced have gone to this little book for their personal blessing. Rutherford did, McCheyne did, and the most practical evangelist the world has ever seen, Dwight L. Moody, did. In fact, the Song of Solomon was Moody's favorite book. My friend, why don't you read it in quietness and let the Spirit of God speak to your heart beyond and above the human affection that is set before us here. The apostle John put it succinctly, "We love Him because He first loved us" (1 John 4:19). What a wonderful thing! And may I say to you, that's what

Christianity is. "We love Him because He first loved us." This little book, if you let it, will break an alabaster box of ointment that will sweeten your life and give a fragrance to your marriage and your testimony. It's a lovely thing!

The Setting

Antiphonal singing was often used by the Hebrews, and the Song of Solomon was written as an antiphon. We hear the bride and the daughters of Jerusalem, one singing a question and the other answering back in song. Then we have the antiphonal singing between the bride and the bridegroom.

There are two scenes in this book. One has a country setting, and the other is in the city. The country scene is north, up in the hill country of Ephraim. We cannot pinpoint the place that is mentioned, and I think the location was obscured purposely. The other scene is in Jerusalem. The one in the country is a scene of poverty. The one in Jerusalem is in the palace. Back and forth the scene shifts. The story looks back upon events and experiences that have already transpired, as the mind of the writer, Solomon, skips back and forth—because it is not in the language of logic but the language of love. And I want you to see that. I trust the Spirit of God will enable us figuratively to remove the shoes from our feet because we are standing on holy ground.

Here is the setting that I consider to be the very key to the book, although it appears in the last chapter, verse 11:

> **Solomon had a vineyard at Baal Hamon;**
> **He leased the vineyard to keepers;**
> **Everyone was to bring for its fruit**
> **A thousand silver coins.**

This sets the stage for the love story. It concerned a farm family who were what we call in the South sharecroppers. They had rented a vineyard of Solomon's, and they had the responsibility of taking care of it, receiving in return a certain amount for their labors. They were tenant farmers, and they were poor. However, we do not have here Steinbeck's *The Grapes of Wrath*, but rather Solomon's grapes of love.

Will you notice verse 12 of the final chapter:

> **My own vineyard is before me.**
> **You, O Solomon, may have a thousand,**
> **And those who tend its fruit two hundred.**

This family kept one of the many vineyards of Solomon. They were an Ephrathite family—Shulamites they were called. Since they lived in the hill country, I think maybe you could have called them hillbillies. We presume the father was not living since he wasn't mentioned here at all. There were in the family a mother, two daughters, and two or more sons. The eldest daughter was—well, we could call her a Cinderella, and she was beautiful, if you please. Listen to her language:

> **Do not look upon me, because I am dark,**
> **Because the sun has tanned me.**
> **My mother's sons were angry with me;**
> **They made me the keeper of the vineyards,**
> **But my own vineyard I have not kept.**
> (Song of Solomon 1:6)

Her brothers made her responsible for maintaining the vineyards. They really worked this girl! And she tells us that she's sunburned. Listen to her in chapter 1, verse 5:

> **I am dark, but lovely,**
> **O daughters of Jerusalem,**
> **Like the tents of Kedar,**
> **Like the curtains of Solomon.**

Now times have changed a great deal in our day. But back in those days a woman with a suntan was looked down upon because it meant she worked out of doors, which, in that time was a disgrace. A lady with light, soft skin stayed inside the home; therefore, that was the thing to be desired. How different from our culture! People will lie under the sun, pour on oil as they sizzle and fry and burn in order that they might get deeply tanned. But in the days of Solomon it was a disgrace, and this girl says, "I know I'm suntanned, but it's because I work outside. My brothers make me take care of the vineyard, and my own vineyard I have not kept up." In other words, "I've never been able to go to a beauty salon, I haven't been able to preserve my own beauty because I've had to keep this vineyard of Solomon's." We can be sure she had a natural loveliness, however, and was a beautiful girl.

Not only did her brothers make her keep the vineyard, but they also made her take care of the flock. When she got through working in the vineyard she had to go out and herd the sheep.

> **If you do not know, O fairest among women,**
> **Follow in the footsteps of the flock,**
> **And feed your little goats**
> **Beside the shepherds' tents.** (1:8)

The brothers kept this girl very busy. The family lived, apparently, on or near the caravan route that led from Jerusalem to Damascus. As she watched the caravans go by, here was her impression:

> **Who is this coming out of the wilderness**
> **Like pillars of smoke,**
> **Perfumed with myrrh and frankincense,**
> **With all the merchant's fragrant powders?**
> (3:6)

She would see these ladies of the court, well dressed and adorned with their jewels and their ointments. This little girl, watching from the sidelines as she worked in the hot sun in the vineyard, was painfully conscious of her own appearance: "I'm suntanned— my own vineyard I have not kept." As she looked at these beautiful ladies with their jewels and their silks, this girl dreamed.

Then one day while she was tending her sheep a handsome shepherd appeared, and he fell in love with her. His words make that clear.

> **Like a lily among thorns,**
> **So is my love among the daughters.** (2:2)

In other words, "I've been looking all my life for *you*, I've never seen anyone like you. To me you are a lily among thorns." He was definitely in love with her. Notice again in the fourth chapter, verse 1:

> **Behold, you are fair, my love!**
> **Behold, you are fair!**

You say, "Well, he's repeating himself." So what? Can you think of anything nicer to say than that? Can you improve upon it? He said to her, "To me you are fair" and emphasized it in verse 7 of chapter 4:

> **You are all fair, my love,**
> **And there is no spot in you.**

He was saying, "To me, you are perfect." If you are a wife, you may remember when your husband first said that to you. Maybe you ought to remind him of it when he says less complimentary things to you now!

What Does It Mean?

May I pause at this point to say once again that I trust you have realized this song is a beautiful picture of the love of Christ for His own, His church. How beautiful. Oh, I know, when you and I look at ourselves and at others in the church we see all of us filled with faults, and some of us are very critical, aren't we? But do you know that when our Lord looks at the church today He doesn't see it that way—He sees it as being altogether lovely. He sees it as the church that He purchased with His own blood, and He has put down over us His robe of righteousness. Let me draw your attention, as in previous chapters, to something wonderful written by the apostle Paul:

Husbands, love your wives, just as Christ also loved the church and gave Himself for her, that He might sanctify and cleanse her with the washing of water by the word . . .

Now notice,

. . . that He might present her to Himself a glorious church, not having spot or wrinkle or any such thing, but that she should be holy and without blemish. (Ephesians 5:25–27)

That's His church that He will present to Himself someday. You have no notion at this moment—and I don't either—of how much He loves His church. Husbands ought to be careful of criticizing their own wives, and we also need to be careful of criticizing another Man's wife, for the church is our Lord's bride-to-be. He says the church is without spot and wrinkle. Immediately the thought comes to mind, "Well, then, He doesn't know me, and He doesn't know you." But He *does* know us! My friend, He doesn't see you as you are. When you came to Him and trusted Him as Savior, He not only forgave you for your sins, but He also put down over you His robe of righteousness, which is spotless and will enable you to stand in His presence! I suggest that you read for yourself in this Song of Solomon what He says about the bride. He says,

You have ravished my heart, . . .
How fair is your love. (4:9, 10)

Oh, how Christ *loves* the church! Paul found that out, and it broke his heart. Paul had hated Jesus Christ! Oh, how he hated Him and persecuted His disciples. In fact, Paul was responsible for the first martyr and called himself the chiefest of sinners. In my own mind I am sure that Paul stood, along with the chief priests, at the cross on that day of the Crucifixion and shot out the lip at Him and ridiculed Him saying, "If You are the Son of God, come down from the cross" (Matthew 27:40).

Then came the day on the Damascus road when Paul met Him. It was then that Paul found out how much Jesus Christ loved *him*. Listen to him as he relived again the Crucifixion. "He loved me, He gave Himself for me!" (Galatians 2:20). Can you ask Him to do anything more for you to show His love? Paul said, "He loved me." John says, "We love Him because He first loved us" (1 John 4:19). And it's Peter who said, "Whom having not seen, you love" (1 Peter 1:8). God pity the man who is married to a cold and indifferent wife. But what about the Savior this day who has poured out His love and affection on His beloved, and He has only a bunch of cold and indifferent saints who are unresponsive to that love!

Have *you* ever told Him that you love Him? I had not until I was a senior in seminary—I did not realize the extent of His love until then. One night a fellow student, Allen Fleece, and I were walking back to the seminary together. We had just met and were talking excitedly. Suddenly we stopped. The moon, that Georgia moon, was just rising over the crest of another red clay hill as we stood there and watched it. I must confess that tears began to trickle from my eyes, and from Allen's, too. Finally Allen said, "*He* made that!" After a time of silence he added, "Every night when I go to bed, the last thing I do as I pull up the cover is to just look up and say 'Lord Jesus, I love You.'" I thought it was a good idea, so it became my custom also. My friend, when was the last time you told Him that you loved Him? Look, He isn't concerned how busy you are in the church, how many committees you're on, or whether you are a member of the board. He doesn't care today how active you may be in Christian service. He doesn't even care whether you are a preacher or not. But He would like to know whether you *love*

Him or not. Loving Him is the acid test of the level of intimacy you enjoy with the Savior—not *faith* but *love*. Do you love Him? Only when we truly love Him can we love our husband or wife as we should.

He Is Coming Again

Now again, picking up the thread of Solomon's lovely story, we take another look at this very peculiar shepherd. He didn't seem to have any sheep and one day she asked him,

> **Tell me, O you whom I love,**
> **Where you feed your flock,**
> **Where you make it rest at noon. . . .** (1:7a)

In essence his answer to her was, "You don't need to ask any questions, you just trust me." And then he came to her one day and said, "I'm going away for a while but I will come back, and when I come back I will make you my bride." Then he left. Days went by. They lengthened into weeks, even months. Her family began to ridicule her, "Where's that shepherd you've been talking about? What happened to your shepherd? Isn't he coming back for you?" The neighbors began to talk and say unkind things.

Around two thousand years ago, our Lord returned to His throne in heaven. But we read in John 14 that before He left He said, "Don't let your heart be troubled. I'm going to prepare a place for you in My Father's house. Since I am going to prepare a place for you, I will come back and receive you to

Myself; that where I am, there you may be also"
(my paraphrase).

And, friend, we're living in the time period of
which Peter wrote,

> **Knowing this first: that scoffers will come in
> the last days, walking according to their own
> lusts, and saying, "Where is the promise of
> His coming? For since the fathers fell asleep,
> all things continue as they were from the
> beginning of creation."** (2 Peter 3:3–4)

"Where is this Jesus you're talking about? Do you
mean to tell me that you're one of those fanatics
who believe He's going to come back to this earth
again?" Our Lord said, "I am coming back."

Well, Solomon had made that promise to this
naive country girl, and she trusted him. She loved
him. She actually dreamed of him:

> **By night on my bed I sought the one I love;
> I sought him, but I did not find him.** (3:1)

And one night she lay restless on the couch when
she smelled a fragrance and knew he had been near.
And this is what happened.

> **I arose to open for my beloved,
> And my hands dripped with myrrh,
> My fingers with liquid myrrh,
> On the handles of the lock.** (5:5)

The custom in that day was when a man was engaged
to a girl and wanted her to know how much he really
loved her, he would slip over at night to her home,
and since the handle of the door was on the inside

where there was an opening (they didn't have Yale locks then like we have today), he would reach through to the inside and put myrrh on the handles of the door. Then when she would come and open it, she would get myrrh on her hands, and the fragrance would fill the home.

So this particular night when she smelled the fragrance of myrrh and knew her beloved was near, she got up from bed and went to the door. She said, "My fingers dripped with liquid myrrh." She knew he'd been there, and she knew he would come for her someday.

Our Lord told us, ". . . Lo, I am with you always, even to the end of the age" (Matthew 28:20). When Paul was arrested he was put into the Mamertine prison, that dark, dank dungeon in Rome. And if you would have gone there, as many believers did, to sympathize with him and say, "Poor Paul, it's awful to be in this stench and darkness," I have a notion he would have said, "No, you're wrong. Last night this dungeon was filled with a sweet-smelling fragrance." You would sniff and say, "That's not what I smell!" Paul would explain, "The Lord stood by me. He was here, and His fragrance filled the place."

My friend, today the essence of the Christian life is to live in the presence of Jesus Christ. It's to have the fragrance of His person in our lives—in the workplace, the marketplace, and especially in our homes. Again, let me repeat it: The real test of your Christian life is not faith—that's the way you got saved. And the real test today is not your service, not your sacrifice, not your gifts. But the real test is *love*. Do *you* love Him? Paul in 1 Corinthians 13 said,

> **Though I speak with the tongues of men and of angels, but have not love, I have become sounding brass or a clanging cymbal. . . . And though I give my body to be burned, but have not love, it profits me nothing. . . . And now abide faith, hope, love, these three; but the greatest of these is love.** (verses 1, 3, 13)

Is Jesus Christ at this moment real to you? I didn't ask you if you are a member of a Bible-teaching church. How real is Jesus Christ Himself to you today? He asks the question, "Do you love Me?" He said to the church in Ephesus, "Nevertheless I have this against you, that you have left your first love" (Revelation 2:4). I wonder if He would say that to your church and to mine. Oh, we're busy in our churches and interested in missions, but have we left our first love? Is there the fragrance of Christ in your life today?

Dr. Albert Dudley was a wonderful man. I followed him in my first pastorate, and what a blessing it was to be guided by a man like that. This man comforted my heart. After he had retired he said to me one day when I dropped by to see him, "Vernon, last night I couldn't sleep. I had been studying the Book of Ezekiel." (Imagine a retired minister studying! Never till his dying day did he give up searching the Scriptures.) Then he told me his experience: "I was thinking last night about that glory, that Shekinah glory which Ezekiel saw."

He said again, "Don't misunderstand me—I'm not seeing visions, and there was nothing visible in my room—but the glory was so real to me and the presence of Christ so real that finally I slipped out of bed, got down on my knees and said, 'O Lord, turn it off; I can't stand anymore!'" Have you ever been that close to Him?

Well, one day the bride-to-be was busy in the vineyard. She was out there, probably trying to catch the foxes:

> **The little foxes that spoil the vines,**
> **For our vines have tender grapes.**
> (Song of Solomon 2:15)

Maybe she was out setting fox traps, just as busy as she could be, when down the road there came a cry, "The king is coming! He's coming!"

> **Who is this coming out of the wilderness**
> **Like pillars of smoke,**
> **Perfumed with myrrh and frankincense,**
> **With all the merchant's fragrant powders?**
> **Behold, it is Solomon's couch,**
> **With sixty valiant men around it,**
> **Of the valiant of Israel.**
> **They all hold swords,**
> **Being expert in war.**
> **Every man has his sword on his thigh**
> **Because of fear in the night.**
> **Of the wood of Lebanon**
> **Solomon the King**
> **Made himself a palanquin** [an enclosed couch borne on the shoulders of servants]. (3:6–9)

And here he came in that fancy palanquin! Everybody was excited and rushed to the roadside, and somebody said to her, "Aren't you coming?"

"No, I'm not interested."

"You mean you're not interested in King Solomon passing by?"

"No." She was preoccupied with her work and thoughts of the one she loved. And while she was still busy at the vineyard there came up to her a servant who said, "King Solomon wants to see you."

"Me? He doesn't know me."

"Yes, King Solomon wants to see you."

"Why? He couldn't possibly know about me."

"Well, you'll have to come." And so they took her along. When she came into the presence of King Solomon she bowed, and when she looked up, she found herself looking into the face of her shepherd!

He has come now. He came the first time as a shepherd. He has come again as a king. This was beyond her expectation, and it was finally her experience. Listen to her:

The voice of my beloved!
Behold, he comes
Leaping upon the mountains,
Skipping upon the hills.
My beloved is like a gazelle or a young stag.
Behold, he stands behind our wall;
He is looking through the windows,
Gazing through the lattice.
My beloved spoke, and said to me:
"Rise up, my love, my fair one,
And come away.

For lo, the winter is past,
The rain is over and gone.
The flowers appear on the earth;
The time of singing has come,
And the voice of the turtledove
Is heard in our land.
The fig tree puts forth her green figs,
And the vines with the tender grapes
Give a good smell.
Rise up, my love, my fair one,
And come away!" (2:8–13)

Then listen to him in verse 14: "O my dove . . ."—the church is to be as harmless as a dove and as wise as a serpent—"in the clefts of the rock," and that's where His believers are hidden today, secured by the shed blood of Christ. As someone has well said, "I got into the heart of Christ through a spear wound." In the secret places of the cliffs His own have access to Him. Notice what He wants from us: "Let me see your face, let me hear your voice." And, my friend, our Lord wants to see you before He hears you. He wants you close to Him. "For your voice is sweet, and your face is lovely."

Beloved, the expectation and hope of every believer today is just simply this: He says, "My sheep hear My voice, and I know them, and they follow Me" (John 10:27). One of these days His voice is to sound, "For the Lord Himself will descend from heaven with a shout, with the voice of an archangel, and with the trumpet of God. . ." (1 Thessalonians 4:16). Even the dead in Christ are going to hear Him and, together with those who are alive, they are to be caught up and presented to Him as the bride that

He loved and for whom He gave Himself! Will you listen to Him now?

O my dove, in the clefts of the rock,
In the secret places of the cliff,
Let me see your face,
Let me hear your voice;
For your voice is sweet,
And your face is lovely. (Song of Solomon 2:14)

It has been said that the Song of Solomon does not have a climax. I disagree with that. It has the same climax with which the New Testament closes the Bible. Notice the last verse of Solomon's song:

Make haste, my beloved,
And be like a gazelle
Or a young stag
On the mountains of spices.

She says, "Make haste, my beloved." The New Testament closes the Bible with the prayer, "And the Spirit and the bride say, 'Come!' . . . He who testifies to these things says, 'Surely I am coming quickly.' Amen. Even so, come, Lord Jesus!" (Revelation 22:17, 20). That's the climax of the Bible. And, friend, it's the climax this moment of your faith and my faith of our love for Him and His love for us. Even so, make haste, come, my Beloved.

CHAPTER 10

BEHOLD, OUR BRIDEGROOM COMES!

One of the most familiar chapters in the Bible is probably John 14, and most familiar of all its verses are 1 through 3:

> **Let not your heart be troubled; you believe in God, believe also in Me. In My Father's house are many mansions; if it were not so, I would have told you. I go to prepare a place for you. And if I go and prepare a place for you, I will come again and receive you to Myself; that where I am, there you may be also.**

There is something special here, a marvelous truth to dwell on. We need to understand what the Lord Jesus really has in mind when He uses the language that we read here. He bases it on the background of a Jewish wedding in His day, and it involves a groom and his bride. Actually, I've felt for years that the Rapture was there, but I never could put my finger on it.

The Betrothal Ceremony

Although there are many figures that explain the relationship of Christ and His church, one that is frequently used is the bridegroom and the bride.

As we look at the implications of God's overall plan in the ceremonies of a Jewish wedding in Jesus' day, perhaps we can comprehend His high standard for marriage in the church, and let the glory sift on down to our day and relationships in the home. You'll find that Paul the apostle, in writing to the Corinthians, said,

For I am jealous for you with godly jealousy. For I have betrothed you to one husband, that I may present you as a chaste virgin to Christ. (2 Corinthians 11:2)

"I have betrothed you" is a figure of speech that Paul used—"I am making you engaged," as it were. "I am bringing you into a personal relationship with the Lord Jesus Christ."

You'll find that John, in the Book of Revelation, used that same figure of speech. After you get through reading about all of that Great Tribulation period, you find that the bride is in heaven, and John wrote, "The marriage of the Lamb has come" (Revelation 19:7).

And James, that very practical apostle, used it in a negative way. He said,

Adulterers and adulteresses! Do you not know that friendship with the world is enmity with God? Whoever therefore wants to be a friend of the world makes himself an enemy of God. (James 4:4)

In other words, he likens a believer's unfaithfulness to Christ to committing adultery! Therefore, we need to understand the customs of a Jewish wedding in Jesus' day in order to understand what He's talking about in John 14. I am deeply indebted to Dr. Renald Showers of the Philadelphia College of the Bible who has done some very fine research in this connection and has made it available to me.

Now I want you to notice what a Jewish wedding was like in the first century in the days of our Lord. It was not a day when the bride brought a dowry with her to the marriage. The fact of the matter is, that was not a Bible custom but one that came along much later. After all, what was the dowry that Eve brought to Adam? She did not bring a dowry to him at all—she brought herself. And I think she was probably the most wonderful woman who has ever been on this earth.

In a first-century marriage, the initial step was taken by the young man who had fallen in love with some girl. What happened was this: When he'd fallen in love with the girl and knew that she would marry him, he traveled from his father's house to the girl's home, and he bargained with the father of the girl about how much he would pay for her. The purchase price that he was to pay for his bride was called a *mohar*, and when the amount of the mohar was mutually satisfactory to the father and also to the young man, then the young lady was consulted. If it was also satisfactory with her, a marriage covenant was made. The bride was then declared to be sanctified. And that means only that she was set apart for the bridegroom. That is the picture we have at the opening of the New Testament; Mary was espoused to Joseph, which tells us they had already gone through the betrothal service.

Now this betrothal service was actually like a marriage ceremony. It was concluded by the prospective bridegroom and bride taking a glass of wine and each drinking from it. She was now espoused to him. Then when the betrothal benediction was pronounced, the young man returned to his father's house to prepare a place for his bride. During this time, the bride-to-be prepared herself to become a bride and to enter married life.

This was the first stage, and I'm sure that by now you've recognized the parallel to Christ and His church. Almost two thousand years ago He left the ivory palaces of heaven. He left His Father's house and came to our house—this world in which you and I live—to seek His bride. He gives us this tremendous movement in John 16:28, and many expositors consider this verse to be the key to John's Gospel. And they are not far amiss, by the way. The Lord Jesus said,

I came forth from the Father and have come into the world. Again, I leave the world and go to the Father.

What a tremendous movement: out of the glories of heaven and down to this earth for just a brief period of time. John Wesley put it like this: "God contracted to a span." And then, having made the engagement down here, He goes back to heaven to prepare a place for His bride.

That's the picture you have in John's Gospel. He opened with,

In the beginning was the Word, and the Word was with God, and the Word was God. He was in the beginning with God. (John 1:1–2)

And then the Word began to move, and in John 1:14 we find, "And the Word became flesh and dwelt among us," or the Word was born flesh and He pitched His tent (that is, a body), His human tent, here among us. He became one of us when He came down to this earth. And then John continues,

No one has seen God at any time. The only begotten Son, who is in the bosom of the Father, He has declared Him. (John 1:18)

"Declared Him," *exegeomai,* means "exegeted Him." He has let Him out where men can see God for the first time. And the Lord Jesus said to Philip in John 14:9, "He who has seen Me has seen the Father."

Christ was 100 percent God! And the writer to the Hebrews came along and said,

> **But we see Jesus, who was made a little lower than the angels, for the suffering of death crowned with glory and honor, that He, by the grace of God, might taste death for everyone.** (Hebrews 2:9)

And then farther down in that chapter he said,

> **For indeed He does not give aid to angels, but He does give aid to the seed of Abraham. Therefore, in all things He had to be made like His brethren, that He might be a merciful and faithful High Priest in things pertaining to God, to make propitiation for the sins of the people.** (Hebrews 2:16–17)

Now that is the wonderful, glorious picture of the Lord Jesus coming from the Father's house down to our house and becoming a man.

And when Christ came down here, He paid a price for His bride. He explains that price in Mark 10:45:

> **For even the Son of Man did not come to be served, but to serve, and to give His life a ransom for many.**

He paid a price for you and me. That word *ransom* went out of the English language for a long time. It was not in our vocabulary; you didn't hear anything about it, and they tried to get rid of it. But believe me, the kidnappers have really put it back in use again. One rich child after another has been kidnapped, and a ransom has been demanded.

I remember when Mr. Getty's grandson was kidnapped. Mr. Getty was supposed to be the richest man in the world and they demanded a tremendous ransom. They showed a picture of that boy on TV, and as I looked at him, I realized that millions were paid for that boy! I began to think about the fact that I had been ransomed also, and a tremendous price was paid for me. And if you want to know something, I was not worthy. I like the song that reminds me that, "I am not worthy the least of His favor, but Jesus left heaven for me." I wasn't worth it, and neither were you. Someone has said that if we could see ourselves as God sees us, we wouldn't be able to stand ourselves. My friend, what a price was paid for you and me! We were alienated from God. Paul said to the Ephesians, "You were without hope and without God in the world. Dead in trespasses and sins." But Jesus came down and paid a price, and what price did He pay? Peter tells us in 1 Peter 1:18 and 19,

> **Knowing that you were not redeemed with corruptible things, like silver or gold, from your aimless conduct received by tradition from your fathers, but with the precious blood of Christ, as of a lamb without blemish and without spot.**

My, He paid a tremendous price!

Our Lord sealed the betrothal in the Upper Room. There on the dying embers of a fading feast, the

Passover, He raised up a new feast. And after the cup had passed for the Passover, He took up the cup again, and He said, as Paul put it,

In the same manner He also took the cup after supper, saying, "This cup is the new covenant in My blood. This do, as often as you drink it, in remembrance of Me." (1 Corinthians 11:25)

He took the cup that night on which He was betrayed, just a few hours before He was arrested; and the next day He was brought before Pilate and crucified. But four days after the night in the Upper Room, He rose from the dead! He had said in effect, "This cup is a new covenant; in other words, with My blood I will pay a price for you." That's a betrothal! And, my friend, when you go to the Lord's table—and I wish Christians today had a higher view of the Lord's table than they do—when you and I take that cup, we are responding to Him, and we're saying to Him, "We belong to You. You paid a price for us. You have redeemed us." It is a pledge of allegiance to Him when we take that cup. In the Upper Room He took the cup that spoke of His blood that He would shed to pay for your redemption and my redemption. And now when you and I take the cup, it's a pledge on our part.

I don't know about you, but I'm so tired of cheap Christianity today! I'm tired of seeing people play church. I'm so weary of shoddy sanctification, and I'm tired of hearing about dead dedication. I hear so many people say, "I'm dedicated to Christ." You're not dedicated to Him unless you're married to Him, unless you're joined to Him. My, how low we've let this thing sink in our day.

Now will you notice, after the Jewish bridegroom had made the pledge, he went back to his father's house. And the Lord Jesus said here,

In my Father's house are many mansions; if it were not so, I would have told you. I go to prepare a place for you. (John 14:2)

And based on the background of the weddings and their customs of that day, He makes this statement to every believer, "I'm putting you in the body of believers, in the church. That church is to be My bride. And I'm coming someday for My bride, but right now I am preparing a place for you. In My Father's house there are many mansions." Actually, I don't like the term mansions. I lived for many years (well not too many, it just *seemed* long) in what the Presbyterian denomination called a *manse*. They put their preacher in this manse, which is a short form for mansion. And I have lived in some most unusual mansions in my day.

When I went to my first church in Nashville, Tennessee, the old manse there was an antebellum home with fourteen rooms in it. I used to tell the folk that on a clear day, you could see the ceiling in the living room. It was a big thing, and I can remember that on a cold day all I had was a little fireplace in which I burned coal. I'd roast on one side and freeze on the other, then I'd turn around and reverse the process. So when somebody tells me that I'm going to have a mansion over there, well, may I say to you, it leaves me cold. I don't want it. I don't want a mansion. And I thank God that's not what He really said. He said, "In My Father's house are many *mone*." *Mone* doesn't mean mansion any more than it means a doghouse. It has only one meaning, "abiding place."

What does He mean when He says, "In My Father's house"? Well, when you go outside at night and look up and see the stars, you'll be looking into my Father's house. That's His house, up there. It's a big house, and He says there are many abiding places in it.

When our Lord said that, man did know a little something about our solar system. The Egyptians knew the distance to the sun, and they knew we were in a solar system, but they knew nothing about what was beyond. And later Galileo came along with a telescope, and they discovered that beyond our planetary system there are other planetary systems and that all together we form a galactic system. And then they made better telescopes, and they found out that beyond our galactic system there are other galactic systems. Then they discovered that beyond the galactic systems there's something else, and with the great big dish that they had up here on the Mojave Desert, they found out that there are systems way out there that they call *quasars*. I asked a friend of mine, "Why do you call them quasars?" He said, "*Quasar* is a German word. It means that you don't know what it is." But it sounds scientific, you know, to say those are quasars. And when I use that word, somebody says,

"My, isn't that preacher smart. He knows what those are." But when you say quasar, what you are really saying is, "I don't know what it is." Then the British had a bigger dish and they found something beyond the quasars. The British always come up with a good one, so they called them *black holes*. And that, my friend, is the best scientific term yet—*black holes*!

The Lord Jesus said that night, "In My Father's house there are many abiding places, but I go to prepare a place for you." The Bridegroom has gone back to the Father's house to prepare a place for the bride. And one of these days He's coming.

When Will He Return for the Bride?

Now that brings us to the second phase of a first-century marriage. When the bridegroom returned to his father's house to prepare a place for the bride, he did not come back for her immediately. It was at least a year. It could be even less, but generally a year or more. And the time of his coming was something that the bride knew nothing about. No date was ever set for his return; no advance word was given. The bride was to wait in anticipation, in expectation and preparation. And that leads me now to say again that we are not given any sign today about the Rapture of the church! None whatsoever—any more than this bride was told when the bridegroom would return.

She did not know. She was to *anticipate* his coming; she was to *expect* it; she was to *prepare* for it. Then one day, at the time decided upon by the bridegroom and by him alone, he came to take the bride to live with him. It was generally at night, and male escorts came with him. And when he got within earshot of the home of the bride, he shouted—that was the first inkling and the first indication she had that he was coming!

When somebody tries to tell me that the Lord Jesus is coming soon—that's very unscriptural. He never said that. But didn't He say, "Behold, I come quickly"? That is in the Book of the Revelation, and He is saying that all those great events outlined in the Revelation are going to happen quickly, in rapid succession. That's all it means. He didn't say, "I'm coming soon." If He did say that, I don't know what He could have meant because almost two thousand years have passed. But when the bridegroom in that first-century wedding got near the house, he shouted, and the shout announced his arrival. This was the *first*, let me repeat it, the *first* indication or inkling that the bride had that her beloved was coming. He didn't write a letter saying he would be there on a certain date. He did not send some sensational preacher to announce the date and say, "Now that the planets have all gotten in line with Jupiter, it means that the bridegroom is coming." He never did any of that.

Nor did our Lord say, "Because Israel is back in the land, I will be coming soon." He didn't tell us to write a book, setting dates for His coming. It'll sure sell books, but He won't be there on that day. And He won't come on the date that any person in any book predicts.

And, notice this carefully, the Bible does not say the King is coming! There's more wrong theology given in songs today than in almost any other way. I wish songwriters would study their Bibles a little more before they write songs. He didn't say, "The King is coming!" He said, "Behold, the bridegroom is coming" (Matthew 25:6). And Christ is coming as the Bridegroom to take His church out *before* He comes to this earth to establish His Kingdom.

Will you give close attention to Him now? He says, "If I go and prepare a place for you, I will come again and receive you to Myself; that where I am, there you may be also" (John 14:3). And on that basis Paul wrote in Ephesians:

Husbands, love your wives, just as Christ also loved the church and gave Himself for her, that He might sanctify and cleanse her with the washing of water by the word, that He might present her to Himself a glorious church, not having spot or wrinkle or any such thing, but that she should be holy and without blemish. (Ephesians 5:25–27)

Someone who hears me by radio wrote, "I don't think you believe in holiness." Well, if by that he means perfection, I don't believe in it down here, because I don't see any of it down here. But one of these days I'm going to be holy and perfect—"without spot or wrinkle." Boy, won't that be a day to look at Vernon McGee!

The Bridegroom will have a holy bride. In Revelation 19, John again picks this up. He said,

> **Let us be glad and rejoice and give Him glory, for the marriage of the Lamb has come, and His wife has made herself ready.** (Revelation 19:7)

How did she make herself ready? Look at the next verse:

> **And to her it was granted to be arrayed in fine linen, clean and bright, for the fine linen is the righteous acts of the saints.** (Revelation 19:8)

At the Rapture we will be brought into the presence of Christ, and rewards will be given for service to Him. That is going to be a wonderful day. And then we will be reunited with our loved ones (see 2 Samuel 12:22–23). Won't it be wonderful to see other believers that we have loved—like the one who led us to Christ? Won't it be wonderful to see that little child that you lost? Won't it be wonderful to see that husband or that wife and perhaps Mother and Dad (see 1 Thessalonians 4:17)? That reunion is going to take place following the Rapture. And after that, the wonderful thing that is going to happen is the marriage. I believe the marriage will take place in heaven, and a little later the marriage supper will be on earth.

Home at Last!

The next step in the Jewish marriage was when the bridegroom took the bride to his home. He took her to the room that he had prepared, called the *huppah*. That's where the Lord Jesus is going to take His bride to give out the rewards. He will review your life and my life someday.

And the friends who were with the bridegroom would wait on the outside. That's what John the Baptist meant when he said, "He who has the bride is the bridegroom." You see, they asked him if he was the Messiah. He said, "He who has the bride is the bridegroom; but the friend of the bridegroom, who stands and hears him, rejoices greatly because of the bridegroom's voice. Therefore this joy of mine is fulfilled" (John 3:29). John the Baptist was never in the church. He is the last of the Old Testament prophets, and he introduced the Lord Jesus. He said, "I'm not the bridegroom. I don't have the bride. But I am a friend of the bridegroom." John the Baptist is going to be at the marriage of the Lamb.

Now after the bride and bridegroom have been together in the *huppah*, the bridegroom comes out and announces that there has been the physical consummation of the wedding. Following that, there are seven days of celebration on the part of their friends, but the bride is not revealed during that period at all. Seven days of years of celebration in heaven! Being with our loved ones, and being with the Lord Jesus. I personally can't even conceive how wonderful that is going to be.

But what is taking place on earth during this time? The seven days or seven years of days are the period of tribulation on earth. During this time the bride is hidden in the bride chamber with the Bridegroom! Our Lord made that clear when He wrote to the church in Philadelphia. He said, in Revelation 3:10,

Because you have kept My command to persevere, I also will keep you from the hour of trial which shall come upon the whole world, to test those who dwell on the earth.

Believe me, the amillennialists and the posttribulationists have really had their problems with this verse. And they have gone to great lengths to misinterpret it, but it means exactly what it says. He said, "I'll keep you, the church, from that hour of testing that is coming upon the earth," and you can't get anything else out of it. If that's not enough, in Romans, where Paul mentioned eight wonderful possessions of the church, one of them is this:

Much more then, having now been justified by His blood, we shall be saved from wrath through Him. (Romans 5:9)

And that is the great day of wrath that is coming upon this earth someday. Christ has saved us from that. But if you told me today that I would have to go through the Great Tribulation and I believed you, I wouldn't sleep good tonight. I don't think I could endure it, to begin with, and I thank God that the Tribulation is not my hope. My hope is to hear His voice someday and to go be with Him. He made that very clear to the believers in Thessalonica:

. . . How you turned to God from idols to serve the living and true God, and to wait for His Son from heaven, whom He raised from the dead, even Jesus who delivers us from the wrath to come. (1 Thessalonians 1:9–10)

And the great day of wrath is ahead—the Great Tribulation.

The particular words that God used are interesting. He said to the church, "to wait for His Son from heaven." But in Matthew 24:42 when our Lord is talking to those in the Great Tribulation, He said,

Watch therefore, for you do not know what hour your Lord is coming.

And, my friend, there's a difference between waiting and watching. Somebody says, "Aren't you splitting hairs?" I don't think so. There are seventeen different words used in the Bible that are translated by *wait* or *watch*. And you can wait or watch differently.

Let me give you an illustration. Here's a man who goes deer hunting every year with his neighbor. They get in their camper, they go up to Oregon, and they camp at night. The next morning they get up early and hike to that hogback where they've been every year, where he got his deer last year, and you see him sitting there on a log. He's watching, and he's waiting for that deer with antlers to appear. And God have mercy on any hunter who comes through those bushes—he might get shot too! But that fellow's waiting and watching.

But then you see that man three weeks later, standing here on the corner, and he's looking down this street and he's looking down that street, and you wonder who in the world he is waiting on. So you go up to him and you say, "You look like you're waiting for somebody." He replies, "I am. She's forty-five minutes late already." You see, he's waiting differently for his wife than he waited for that deer. He's waiting for another dear, but it's a different kind of waiting.

Now let's move up a little. It's three months later. You walk into a certain hospital, you go down the hallway, you look in, and you see him and his wife, and they're waiting, waiting at the bedside of a little fellow. The doctor says the crisis will come at midnight. They're waiting. That's an entirely different kind of waiting and watching.

God says to the church today, "You are to wait." That means to wait in expectation, wait in joy— the joy of seeing Him. But He doesn't say "watch" as if it were a fearful thing to do. Those are two altogether different words in the Greek. *Anameno*, meaning "to wait," has in it the idea of patience. "To watch," *gregoreo*, is a Greek word that expresses fearfulness and danger. That's the word used in Matthew 24:42. And Paul in his second letter to Timothy, writing his own epitaph, leaves us with some of his last words:

For I am already being poured out as a drink offering, and the time of my departure is at hand. I have fought the good fight, I have finished the race, I have kept the faith. Finally, there is laid up for me the crown of righteousness, which the Lord, the righteous Judge, will give to me on that Day, and not to me only but also to all who have loved His appearing. (2 Timothy 4:6–8)

My friend, it's a matter of a love relationship. It's not a fearful relationship like, "Oh, I've got to go through the Great Tribulation!" No, it's waiting for and loving His appearing. It's that kind of a personal relationship.

My friend, when you and I come to the Communion service, the Lord says, "This cup is the cup of the new covenant, in My blood," and He adds, "You do this in remembrance of Me, until I come." And probably no one who is a believer in the Lord Jesus Christ will fail to say as he takes that cup, "Even so, come, Lord Jesus." We want to see Him. I belong to Jesus, Jesus belongs to me, and it's a personal relationship. We've been sanctified. That means we have been set apart for Him; we belong to Him!

Dr. Donald Grey Barnhouse did something that was rather sensational. He put together a marriage ritual between Christ and His people. First I want to pass on to you the pledge of the Bridegroom, who is the Lord Jesus, and then the response of the sinner when he comes to Christ.

First, Jesus says to the sinner:

I, Jesus, take thee sinner, to be my bride. And I do promise and covenant before God the Father and these witnesses to be thy loving, faithful Savior and Bridegroom, in sickness and in health, in plenty and in want, in joy and in sorrow, in faithfulness and in waywardness, for time and eternity.

Almost two thousand years ago our Lord took a cup; and knowing that He was to go to the Cross, that He was the Lamb of God slain before the foundation of the world for sinners, He took that cup and He said, "This is My pledge; this is My new covenant, and I will save you if you'll come to Me and trust Me."

Just as a bride says yes to a bridegroom, that's all the Savior asks you or me to say to Him.

Now here is what the sinner is to say:

I, sinner, take Thee, Jesus, to be my Savior; and I do promise and covenant before God and these witnesses to be Thy loving and faithful bride, in sickness and in health, in plenty and in want, for time and for eternity.

Christ is coming personally for His bride. In contrast He will send angels when He comes to establish His Kingdom, and they will gather the elect from everywhere. But He is coming for us Himself, and He's coming with a shout. And when He comes with that shout, as Paul says, that is going to be the bride's first inkling that He has come. When our Lord calls His bride to His home, He will send no letter and will give no signs beforehand at all.

He is coming with a shout, the voice of the archangel, and the trumpet of God. His voice is going to be like the voice of an archangel because of the majesty of it and the dignity of it. But what about the trumpet mentioned in 1 Thessalonians 4:16? His voice is going to be like a trumpet. You say, "Do you know that?" Yes, I know that. When John was exiled on the Isle of Patmos, he wrote, "And I heard behind me a loud voice, as of a trumpet" (Revelation 1:10). Whose voice was it? It was the glorified Christ's. That ought to get rid of this notion today that Gabriel is going to blow a trumpet someday. Oh, my friend, the Lord Jesus said, "My sheep hear *My* voice, and I know them, and they follow Me" (John 10:27, italics added).

One day there will be that shout, and it won't be until then that the bride will know He is coming. No one will know until then. And when we hear that shout, we who are alive and remain will follow those who have already died in Christ, and we'll go with Him into heaven, into the place that He has prepared for those who are His own. That is our hope today! But in the meantime, the reader is brought back to the ordinary routine of Christian living in the home:

> **For we are members of His body, of His flesh and of His bones. "For this reason a man shall leave his father and mother and be joined to his wife, and the two shall become one flesh." This is a great mystery, but I speak concerning Christ and the church. Nevertheless let each one of you in particular so love his own**

wife as himself, and let the wife see that she respects her husband. (Ephesians 5:30–33)

The husband and the wife in the home are to set forth in simplicity the mystery of the coming glory. "Nevertheless" brings us down to earth with a jolt. This is the practical part about marriage. Oh, how sin has marred this glorious relationship—as it has marred everything else—but this relationship can be lifted with the help of the Lord to that high plane and can be yours if you want it to be the best.

NOTES

Chapter 3

1. Robert Browning, "One Word More," in John Bartlett, *Familiar Quotations* (Boston: Little, Brown & Co., 1951), p. 488.

Chapter 4

1. F. W. Farrar, *Life and Work of St. Paul* (New York: Cassel, 1889).

Chapter 5

1. Richard Ellsworth Day, *The Shadow of the Broad Brim—The Life Story of Charles Haddon Spurgeon* (Valley Forge, PA: Judson Press, 1934), p. 104.
2. Walter A. Maier, *For Better Not for Worse*, p. 556.
3. John Lord, *Beacon Lights of History*, Volume VII, Great Women (New York: James Clarke & Co., 1886), pp. 23, 24.
4. Ibid.
5. Nehemiah Carnock, ed. *The Journal of the Rev. John Wesley, A.M.* (London: Epworth Press, 1938).

Chapter 6

1. Alexander Pope, "Essay on Criticism" in John Bartlett, *Familiar Quotations* (Boston, MA: Little, Brown & Co., 1951), p 211.